The Intrusion
Of Jimmy

P. G. Wodehouse

1st WORLD
LIBRARY
Literary Society

The Intrusion Of Jimmy

P. G. Wodehouse

© 1st World Library – Literary Society, 2005
PO Box 2211
Fairfield, IA 52556
www.1stworldlibrary.org
First Edition

LCCN: 2003195070

Softcover ISBN: 1-59540-346-9
Hardcover ISBN: 1-4218-0796-3
eBook ISBN: 1-59540-396-5

Purchase *"The Intrusion Of Jimmy"*
as a traditional bound book at:
www.1stWorldLibrary.org/purchase.asp?ISBN=1-59540-346-9

1st World Library Literary Society is a nonprofit
organization dedicated to promoting literacy by:

- Creating a free internet library accessible from any
  computer worldwide.
- Hosting writing competitions and offering book
  publishing scholarships.

Readers interested in supporting literacy
through sponsorship, donations or
membership please contact:
literacy@1stworldlibrary.org
Check us out at: www.1stworldlibrary.ORG
and start downloading free ebooks today.

The Intrusion Of Jimmy
contributed by the Charles Family
in support of
1st World Library Literary Society

CONTENTS

CHAPTER I

JIMMY MAKES A BET

The main smoking-room of the Strollers' Club had been filling for the last half-hour, and was now nearly full. In many ways, the Strollers', though not the most magnificent, is the pleasantest club in New York. Its ideals are comfort without pomp; and it is given over after eleven o'clock at night mainly to the Stage. Everybody is young, clean-shaven, and full of conversation: and the conversation strikes a purely professional note.

Everybody in the room on this July night had come from the theater. Most of those present had been acting, but a certain number had been to the opening performance of the latest better-than-Raffles play. There had been something of a boom that season in dramas whose heroes appealed to the public more pleasantly across the footlights than they might have done in real life. In the play that had opened to-night, Arthur Mifflin, an exemplary young man off the stage, had been warmly applauded for a series of actions which, performed anywhere except in the theater, would certainly have debarred him from remaining a member of the Strollers' or any other club. In faultless evening dress, with a debonair smile on his face, he had broken open a safe, stolen bonds and jewelry to a large amount, and escaped without a blush of shame via the window. He had foiled a detective through four acts, and held up a band of pursuers with a revolver. A large audience had intimated complete approval throughout.

"It's a hit all right," said somebody through the smoke.

"These near-'Raffles' plays always are," grumbled Willett, who played bluff fathers in musical comedy. "A few years ago, they would have been scared to death of putting on a show with a crook as hero. Now, it seems to me the public doesn't want anything else. Not that they know what they DO want," he concluded, mournfully.

"The Belle of Boulogne," in which Willett sustained the role of Cyrus K. Higgs, a Chicago millionaire, was slowly fading away on a diet of paper, and this possibly prejudiced him.

Raikes, the character actor, changed the subject. If Willett once got started on the wrongs of the ill-fated "Belle," general conversation would become impossible. Willett, denouncing the stupidity of the public, as purely a monologue artiste.

"I saw Jimmy Pitt at the show," said Raikes. Everybody displayed interest.

"Jimmy Pitt? When did he come back? I thought he was in Italy."

"He came on the Lusitania, I suppose. She docked this morning."

"Jimmy Pitt?" said Sutton, of the Majestic Theater. "How long has he been away? Last I saw of him was at the opening of 'The Outsider' at the Astor. That's a couple of months ago."

"He's been traveling in Europe, I believe," said Raikes. "Lucky beggar to be able to. I wish I could."

Sutton knocked the ash off his cigar.

"I envy Jimmy," he said. "I don't know anyone I'd rather be. He's got much more money than any man except a professional 'plute' has any right to. He's as strong as an ox. I shouldn't say he'd ever had anything worse than measles in his life. He's got no relations. And he isn't married."

Sutton, who had been married three times, spoke with some feeling.

"He's a good chap, Jimmy," said Raikes.

"Yes," said Arthur Mifflin, "yes, Jimmy is a good chap. I've known him for years. I was at college with him. He hasn't got my brilliance of intellect; but he has some wonderfully fine qualities. For one thing, I should say he had put more deadbeats on their legs again than half the men in New York put together."

"Well," growled Willett, whom the misfortunes of the Belle had soured, "what's there in that? It's mighty easy to do the philanthropist act when you're next door to a millionaire."

"Yes," said Mifflin warmly, "but it's not so easy when you're getting thirty dollars a week on a newspaper.

When Jimmy was a reporter on the News, there used to be a whole crowd of fellows just living on him. Not borrowing an occasional dollar, mind you, but living on him - sleeping on his sofa, and staying to breakfast. It made me mad. I used to ask him why he stood for it. He said there was nowhere else for them to go, and he thought he could see them through all right - which he did, though I don't see how he managed it on thirty a week."

"If a man's fool enough to be an easy mark - " began Willett.

"Oh, cut it out!" said Raikes. "We don't want anybody knocking Jimmy here."

"All the same," said Sutton, "it seems to me that it was mighty lucky that he came into that money. You can't keep open house for ever on thirty a week. By the way, Arthur, how was that? I heard it was his uncle."

"It wasn't his uncle," said Mifflin. "It was by way of being a romance of sorts, I believe. Fellow who had been in love with Jimmy's mother years ago went West, made a pile, and left it to Mrs. Pitt or her children. She had been dead some time when that happened. Jimmy, of course, hadn't a notion of what was coming to him, when suddenly he got a solicitor's letter asking him to call. He rolled round, and found that there was about five hundred thousand dollars just waiting for him to spend it."

Jimmy Pitt had now definitely ousted "Love, the Cracksman" as a topic of conversation. Everybody present knew him. Most of them had known him in his newspaper days; and, though every man there would have perished rather than admit it, they were grateful to Jimmy for being exactly the same to them now that he could sign a check for half a million as he had been on the old thirty-a-week basis. Inherited wealth, of course, does not make a young man nobler or more admirable; but the young man does not always know this.

"Jimmy's had a queer life," said Mifflin. "He's been pretty much everything in his time. Did you know he was on the stage before he took up newspaper-work? Only on the road, I believe. He got tired of it, and cut it out. That's always been his trouble. He wouldn't settle down to anything. He studied law at Yale, but he never kept it up. After he left the stage, he moved all over the States, without a cent, picking up any odd job he could get. He was a waiter once for a couple of days, but they fired him for breaking plates. Then, he got a job in a jeweler's shop. I believe he's a bit of an expert on jewels. And, another time, he made a hundred dollars by staying three rounds against Kid Brady when the Kid was touring the country after he got the championship away from Jimmy Garwin. The Kid was offering a hundred to anyone who could last three rounds with him. Jimmy did it on his head. He was the best amateur of his weight I ever saw. The Kid wanted him to take up scrapping seriously. But Jimmy wouldn't have stuck to anything long enough in those days. He's one of the gypsies of the world. He was never really happy unless he was on the move, and he doesn't seem to have altered since he came into his money."

"Well, he can afford to keep on the move now," said Raikes. "I wish I - "

"Did you ever hear about Jimmy and - " Mifflin was beginning, when the Odyssey of Jimmy Pitt was interrupted by the opening of the door and the entrance of Ulysses in person.

Jimmy Pitt was a young man of medium height, whose great breadth and depth of chest made him look shorter than he really was. His jaw was square, and protruded slightly; and this, combined with a certain athletic jauntiness of carriage and a pair of piercing brown eyes very much like those of a bull-terrier, gave him an air of aggressiveness, which belied his character. He was not aggressive. He had the good-nature as well as the eyes of a bull-terrier. Also, he possessed, when stirred, all the bull-terrier's dogged determination.

There were shouts of welcome.

"Hullo, Jimmy!"

"When did you get back?"

"Come and sit down. Plenty of room over here."

"Where is my wandering boy tonight?"

"Waiter! What's yours, Jimmy?"

Jimmy dropped into a seat, and yawned.

"Well," he said, "how goes it? Hullo, Raikes! Weren't you at 'Love, the Cracksman'? I thought I saw you. Hullo, Arthur! Congratulate you. You spoke your piece nicely."

"Thanks," said Mifflin. "We were just talking about

you, Jimmy. You came on the Lusitania, I suppose?"

"She didn't break the record this time," said Sutton.

A somewhat pensive look came into Jimmy's eyes.

"She came much too quick for me," he said. "I don't see why they want to rip along at that pace," he went on, hurriedly. "I like to have a chance of enjoying the sea-air."

"I know that sea-air," murmured Mifflin.

Jimmy looked up quickly.

"What are you babbling about, Arthur?"

"I said nothing," replied Mifflin, suavely.

"What did you think of the show tonight, Jimmy?" asked Raikes.

"I liked it. Arthur was fine. I can't make out, though, why all this incense is being burned at the feet of the cracksman. To judge by some of the plays they produce now, you'd think that a man had only to be a successful burglar to become a national hero. One of these days, we shall have Arthur playing Charles Peace to a cheering house."

"It is the tribute," said Mifflin, "that bone-headedness pays to brains. It takes brains to be a successful cracksman. Unless the gray matter is surging about in your cerebrum, as in mine, you can't hope - "

Jimmy leaned back in his chair, and spoke calmly but

with decision.

"Any man of ordinary intelligence," he said, "could break into a house."

Mifflin jumped up and began to gesticulate. This was heresy.

"My good man, what absolute - "

"_I_ could," said Jimmy, lighting a cigarette.

There was a roar of laughter and approval. For the past few weeks, during the rehearsals of "Love, the Cracksman," Arthur Mifflin had disturbed the peace at the Strollers' with his theories on the art of burglary. This was his first really big part, and he had soaked himself in it. He had read up the literature of burglary. He had talked with men from Pinkerton's. He had expounded his views nightly to his brother Strollers, preaching the delicacy and difficulty of cracking a crib till his audience had rebelled. It charmed the Strollers to find Jimmy, obviously of his own initiative and not to be suspected of having been suborned to the task by themselves, treading with a firm foot on the expert's favorite corn within five minutes of their meeting.

"You!" said Arthur Mifflin, with scorn.

"I!"

"You! Why, you couldn't break into an egg unless it was a poached one."

"What'll you bet?" said Jimmy.

The Strollers began to sit up and take notice. The magic word "bet," when uttered in that room, had rarely failed to add a zest to life. They looked expectantly at Arthur Mifflin.

"Go to bed, Jimmy," said the portrayer of cracksmen. "I'll come with you and tuck you in. A nice, strong cup of tea in the morning, and you won't know there has ever been anything the matter with you."

A howl of disapproval rose from the company. Indignant voices accused Arthur Mifflin of having a yellow streak. Encouraging voices urged him not to be a quitter.

"See! They scorn you," said Jimmy. "And rightly. Be a man, Arthur. What'll you bet?"

Mr. Mifflin regarded him with pity.

"You don't know what you're up against, Jimmy," he said. "You're half a century behind the times. You have an idea that all a burglar needs is a mask, a blue chin, and a dark lantern. I tell you he requires a highly specialized education. I've been talking to these detective fellows, and I know. Now, take your case, you worm. Have you a thorough knowledge of chemistry, physics, toxicology - "

"Sure."

" - electricity and microscopy?"

"You have discovered my secret."

"Can you use an oxy-acetylene blow-pipe?"

"I never travel without one."

"What do you know about the administration of anaesthetics?"

"Practically everything. It is one of my favorite hobbies."

"Can you make 'soup'?"

"Soup?"

"Soup," said Mr. Mifflin, firmly.

Jimmy raised his eyebrows.

"Does an architect make bricks?" he said. "I leave the rough preliminary work to my corps of assistants. They make my soup."

"You mustn't think Jimmy's one of your common yeggs," said Sutton. "He's at the top of his profession. That's how he made his money. I never did believe that legacy story."

"Jimmy," said Mr. Mifflin, "couldn't crack a child's money-box. Jimmy couldn't open a sardine-tin."

Jimmy shrugged his shoulders.

"What'll you bet?" he said again. "Come on, Arthur; you're earning a very good salary. What'll you bet?"

"Make it a dinner for all present," suggested Raikes, a canny person who believed in turning the wayside happenings of life, when possible, to his personal profit.

The suggestion was well received.

"All right," said Mifflin. "How many of us are there? One, two, three, four - Loser buys a dinner for twelve."

"A good dinner," interpolated Raikes, softly.

"A good dinner," said Jimmy. "Very well. How long do you give me, Arthur?"

"How long do you want?"

"There ought to be a time-limit," said Raikes. "It seems to me that a flyer like Jimmy ought to be able to manage it at short notice. Why not tonight? Nice, fine night. If Jimmy doesn't crack a crib tonight, it's up to him. That suit you, Jimmy?"

"Perfectly."

Willett interposed. Willett had been endeavoring to drown his sorrows all the evening, and the fact was a little noticeable in his speech.

"See here," he said, "how's J-Jimmy going to prove he's done it?"

"Personally, I can take his word," said Mifflin.

"That be h-hanged for a tale. Wha-what's to prevent him saying he's done it, whether he has or not?"

The Strollers looked uncomfortable. Nevertheless, it

was Jimmy's affair.

"Why, you'd get your dinner in any case," said Jimmy. "A dinner from any host would smell as sweet."

Willett persisted with muddled obstinacy.

"Thash - thash not point. It's principle of thing. Have thish thing square and 'bove board, _I_ say. Thash what _I_ say."

"And very creditable to you being able to say it," said Jimmy, cordially. "See if you can manage 'Truly rural'."

"What _I_ say is - this! Jimmy's a fakir. And what I say is what's prevent him saying he's done it when hasn't done it?"

"That'll be all right," said Jimmy. "I'm going to bury a brass tube with the Stars and Stripes in it under the carpet."

Willett waved his hand.

"Thash quite sh'factory," he said, with dignity. "Nothing more to say."

"Or a better idea," said Jimmy. "I'll carve a big J on the inside of the front door. Then, anybody who likes can make inquiries next day. Well, I'm off home. Glad it's all settled. Anybody coming my way?"

"Yes," said Arthur Mifflin. "We'll walk. First nights always make me as jumpy as a cat. If I don't walk my legs off, I shan't get to sleep tonight at all."

"If you think I'm going to help you walk your legs off, my lad, you're mistaken. I propose to stroll gently home, and go to bed."

"Every little helps," said Mifflin. "Come along."

"You want to keep an eye on Jimmy, Arthur," said Sutton. "He'll sand-bag you, and lift your watch as soon as look at you. I believe he's Arsene Lupin in disguise."

CHAPTER II

PYRAMUS AND THISBE

The two men turned up the street. They walked in silence. Arthur Mifflin was going over in his mind such outstanding events of the evening as he remembered - the nervousness, the relief of finding that he was gripping his audience, the growing conviction that he had made good; while Jimmy seemed to be thinking his own private thoughts. They had gone some distance before either spoke.

"Who is she, Jimmy?" asked Mifflin.

Jimmy came out of his thoughts with a start.

"What's that?"

"Who is she?"

"I don't know what you mean."

"Yes, you do! The sea air. Who is she?"

"I don't know," said Jimmy, simply.

"You don't know? Well, what's her name?"

P.G. Wodehouse

"I don't know."

"Doesn't the Lusitania still print a passenger-list?"

"She does."

"And you couldn't find out her name in five days?"

"No."

"And that's the man who thinks he can burgle a house!" said Mifflin, despairingly.

They had arrived now at the building on the second floor of which was Jimmy's flat.

"Coming in?" said Jimmy.

"Well, I was rather thinking of pushing on as far as the Park. I tell you, I feel all on wires."

"Come in, and smoke a cigar. You've got all night before you if you want to do Marathons. I haven't seen you for a couple of months. I want you to tell me all the news."

"There isn't any. Nothing happens in New York. The papers say things do, but they don't. However, I'll come in. It seems to me that you're the man with the news."

Jimmy fumbled with his latch-key.

"You're a bright sort of burglar," said Mifflin, disparagingly. "Why don't you use your oxy-acetylene blow-pipe? Do you realize, my boy, that you've let yourself in for buying a dinner for twelve hungry men next week? In the cold light of the morning, when reason returns to her throne, that'll come home to you."

"I haven't done anything of the sort," said Jimmy, unlocking the door.

"Don't tell me you really mean to try it."

"What else did you think I was going to do?"

"But you can't. You would get caught for a certainty. And what are you going to do then? Say it was all a joke? Suppose they fill you full of bullet-holes! Nice sort of fool you'll look, appealing to some outraged householder's sense of humor, while he pumps you full of lead with a Colt."

"These are the risks of the profession. You ought to know that, Arthur. Think what you went through tonight."

Arthur Mifflin looked at his friend with some uneasiness. He knew how very reckless Jimmy could be when he had set his mind on accomplishing anything, since, under the stimulus of a challenge, he ceased to be a reasoning being, amenable to argument. And, in the present case, he knew that Willett's words had driven the challenge home. Jimmy was not the man to sit still under the charge of being a fakir, no matter whether his accuser had been sober or drunk.

Jimmy, meanwhile, had produced whiskey and cigars. Now, he was lying on his back on the lounge, blowing smoke-rings at the ceiling.

"Well?" said Arthur Mifflin, at length.

"Well, what?"

"What I meant was, is this silence to be permanent, or are you going to begin shortly to amuse, elevate, and instruct? Something's happened to you, Jimmy. There was a time when you were a bright little chap, a fellow of infinite jest, of most excellent fancy. Where be your gibes now; your gambols, your songs, your flashes of merriment that were wont to set the table in a roar when you were paying for the dinner? Yon remind me more of a deaf-mute celebrating the Fourth of July with noiseless powder than anything else on earth. Wake up, or I shall go. Jimmy, we were practically boys together. Tell me about this girl - the girl you loved, and were idiot enough to lose."

Jimmy drew a deep breath.

"Very well," said Mifflin complacently, "sigh if you like; it's better than nothing."

Jimmy sat up.

"Yes, dozens of times," said Mifflin.

"What do you mean?"

"You were just going to ask me if I had ever been in love, weren't you?"

"I wasn't, because I know you haven't. You have no soul. You don't know what love is."

"Have it your own way," said Mifflin, resignedly.

Jimmy bumped back on the sofa.

"I don't either," he said. "That's the trouble."

Mifflin looked interested.

"I know," he said. "You've got that strange premonitory fluttering, when the heart seems to thrill within you like some baby bird singing its first song, when - "

"Oh, cut it out!"

" - when you ask yourself timidly, 'Is it? Can it really be?' and answer shyly, 'No. Yes. I believe it is!' I've been through it dozens of times; it is a recognized early symptom. Unless prompt measures are taken, it will develop into something acute. In these matters, stand on your Uncle Arthur. He knows."

"You make me sick," Jimmy retorted.

"You have our ear," said Mifflin, kindly. "Tell me all."

"There's nothing to tell."

"Don't lie, James."

"Well, practically nothing."

"That's better."

"It was like this."

"Good."

Jimmy wriggled himself into a more comfortable position, and took a sip from his glass.

"I didn't see her until the second day out."

"I know that second day out. Well?"

"We didn't really meet at all."

"Just happened to be going to the same spot, eh?"

"As a matter of fact, it was like this. Like a fool, I'd bought a second-class ticket."

"What? Our young Rockerbilt Astergould, the boy millionaire, traveling second-class! Why?"

"I had an idea it would be better fun. Everybody's so much more cheery in the second cabin. You get to know people so much quicker. Nine trips out of ten, I'd much rather go second."

"And this was the tenth?"

"She was in the first-cabin," said Jimmy.

Mifflin clutched his forehead.

"Wait!" he cried. "This reminds me of something - something in Shakespeare. Romeo and Juliet? No. I've got it - Pyramus and Thisbe."

"I don't see the slightest resemblance."

"Read your 'Midsummer Night's Dream.' 'Pyramus and Thisbe,' says the story, 'did talk through the chink of a wall,'" quoted Mifflin.

"We didn't."

"Don't be so literal. You talked across a railing."

"We didn't."

"Do you mean to say you didn't talk at all?"

"We didn't say a single word."

Mifflin shook his head sadly.

"I give you up," he said. "I thought you were a man of enterprise. What did you do?"

Jimmy sighed softly.

"I used to stand and smoke against the railing opposite the barber's shop, and she used to walk round the deck."

"And you used to stare at her?"

"I would look in her direction sometimes," corrected Jimmy, with dignity.

"Don't quibble! You stared at her. You behaved like a common rubber-neck, and you know it. I am no prude, James, but I feel compelled to say that I consider your conduct that of a libertine. Used she to walk alone?"

"Generally."

"And, now, you love her, eh? You went on board that

P.G. Wodehouse

ship happy, careless, heart-free. You came off it grave and saddened. Thenceforth, for you, the world could contain but one - woman, and her you had lost."

Mifflin groaned in a hollow and bereaved manner, and took a sip from his glass to buoy him up.

Jimmy moved restlessly on the sofa.

"Do you believe in love at first sight?" he asked, fatuously. He was in the mood when a man says things, the memory of which makes him wake up hot all over for nights to come.

"I don't see what first sight's got to do with it," said Mifflin. "According to your own statement, you stood and glared at the girl for five days without letting up for a moment. I can quite imagine that you might glare yourself into love with anyone by the end of that time."

"I can't see myself settling down," said Jimmy, thoughtfully. "And, until you feel that you want to settle down, I suppose you can't be really in love."

"I was saying practically that about you at the club just before you came in. My somewhat neat expression was that you were one of the gypsies of the world."

"By George, you're quite right!"

"I always am."

"I suppose it's having nothing to do. When I was on the News, I was never like this."

"You weren't on the News long enough to get tired of it."

"I feel now I can't stay in a place more than a week. It's having this money that does it, I suppose."

"New York," said Mifflin, "is full of obliging persons who will be delighted to relieve you of the incubus. Well, James, I shall leave you. I feel more like bed now. By the way, I suppose you lost sight of this girl when you landed?"

"Yes."

"Well, there aren't so many girls in the United States - only twenty million. Or is it forty million? Something small. All you've got to do is to search around a bit. Good-night."

"Good-night."

Mr. Mifflin clattered down the stairs. A minute later, the sound of his name being called loudly from the street brought Jimmy to the window. Mifflin was standing on the pavement below, looking up.

"Jimmy."

"What's the matter now?"

"I forgot to ask. Was she a blonde?"

"What?"

"Was she a blonde?" yelled Mifflin.

"No," snapped Jimmy.

"Dark, eh?" bawled Mifflin, making night hideous.

"Yes," said Jimmy, shutting the window.

"Jimmy!"

The window went up again.

"Well?"

"Me for blondes!"

"Go to bed!"

"Very well. Good-night."

"Good-night."

Jimmy withdrew his head, and sat down in the chair Mifflin had vacated. A moment later, he rose, and switched off the light. It was pleasanter to sit and think in the dark. His thoughts wandered off in many channels, but always came back to the girl on the Lusitania. It was absurd, of course. He didn't wonder that Arthur Mifflin had treated the thing as a joke. Good old Arthur! Glad he had made a success! But was it a joke? Who was it that said, the point of a joke is like the point of a needle, so small that it is apt to disappear entirely when directed straight at oneself? If anybody else had told him such a limping romance, he would have laughed himself. Only, when you are the center of a romance, however limping, you see it from a different angle. Of course, told badly, it was absurd. He could see that. But something away at the back of his mind told him that it was not altogether absurd. And yet - love didn't come like that, in a flash. You might just as well expect a house to spring into being in a moment, or a ship, or an automobile, or a table, or a - He sat up with a jerk. In another instant, he would have been asleep.

He thought of bed, but bed seemed a long way off - the deuce of a way. Acres of carpet to be crawled over, and then the dickens of a climb at the end of it. Besides, undressing! Nuisance - undressing. That was a nice dress the girl had worn on the fourth day out. Tailor-made. He liked tailor-mades. He liked all her dresses. He liked her. Had she liked him? So hard to tell if you don't get a chance of speaking! She was dark. Arthur liked blondes, Arthur was a fool! Good old Arthur! Glad he had made a success! Now, he could marry if he liked! If he wasn't so restless, if he didn't feel that he couldn't stop more than a day in any place! But would the girl have him? If they had never spoken, it made it so hard to -

At this point, Jimmy went to sleep.

P.G. Wodehouse

CHAPTER III

MR. McEACHERN

At about the time when Jimmy's meditations finally merged themselves in dreams, a certain Mr. John McEachern, Captain of Police, was seated in the parlor of his up-town villa, reading. He was a man built on a large scale. Everything about him was large - his hands, his feet, his shoulders, his chest, and particularly his jaw, which even in his moments of calm was aggressive, and which stood out, when anything happened to ruffle him, like the ram of a battle-ship. In his patrolman days, which had been passed mainly on the East side, this jaw of his had acquired a reputation from Park Row to Fourteenth Street. No gang-fight, however absorbing, could retain the undivided attention of the young blood of the Bowery when Mr. McEachern's jaw hove in sight with the rest of his massive person in close attendance. He was a man who knew no fear, and he had gone through disorderly mobs like an east wind.

But there was another side to his character. In fact, that other side was so large that the rest of him, his readiness in combat and his zeal in breaking up public disturbances, might be said to have been only an off-shoot. For his ambition was as large as his fist and as aggressive as his jaw. He had entered the force with the single idea of becoming rich, and had set about achieving his object with a strenuous vigor that was as irresistible as his mighty locust-stick. Some policemen are born grafters, some achieve graft, and some have graft thrust upon them. Mr. McEachern had begun by being the first, had risen to the second, and for some years now had been a prominent member of the small and hugely prosperous third class, the class that does not go out seeking graft, but sits at home and lets graft come to it.

In his search for wealth, he had been content to abide his time. He did not want the trifling sum that every New York policeman acquires. His object was something bigger, and he was prepared to wait for it. He knew that small beginnings were an annoying but unavoidable preliminary to all great fortunes. Probably, Captain Kidd had started in a small way. Certainly, Mr. Rockefeller had. He was content to follow in the footsteps of the masters.

A patrolman's opportunities of amassing wealth are not great. Mr. McEachern had made the best of a bad job. He had not disdained the dollars that came as single spies rather than in battalions. Until the time should arrive when he might angle for whales, he was prepared to catch sprats.

Much may be done, even on a small scale, by perseverance. In those early days, Mr. McEachern's observant eye had not failed to notice certain peddlers who obstructed the traffic, divers tradesmen who did the same by the side-walk, and of restaurant keepers not a few with a distaste for closing at one o'clock in the morning. His researches in this field were not unprofitable. In a reasonably short space of time, he had put by the three thousand dollars that were the price of his promotion to detective-sergeant. He did not like paying three thousand dollars for promotion, but there must be sinking of capital if an investment is to prosper. Mr. McEachern "came across," and climbed one more step up the ladder.

As detective-sergeant, he found his horizon enlarged. There was more scope for a man of parts. Things moved more rapidly. The world seemed full of philanthropists, anxious to "dress his front" and do him other little kindnesses. Mr. McEachern was no churl. He let them dress his front. He accepted the little kindnesses. Presently, he found that he had fifteen thousand dollars to spare for any small flutter that might take his fancy. Singularly enough, this was the precise sum necessary to make him a captain.

He became a captain. And it was then that he discovered that El Dorado was no mere poet's dream, and that Tom Tiddler's Ground, where one might stand picking up gold and silver, was as definite a locality as Brooklyn or the Bronx. At last, after years of patient waiting, he stood like Moses on the mountain, looking down into the Promised Land. He had come to where the Big Money was.

The captain was now reading the little note-book wherein he kept a record of his investments, which were numerous and varied. That the contents were satisfactory was obvious at a glance. The smile on his face and the reposeful position of his jaw were proof enough of that. There were notes relating to house-property, railroad shares, and a dozen other profitable things. He was a rich man.

This was a fact that was entirely unsuspected by his neighbors, with whom he maintained somewhat distant relations, accepting no invitations and giving none. For Mr. McEachern was playing a big game. Other eminent buccaneers in his walk of life had been content to be rich men in a community where moderate means were the rule. But about Mr. McEachern there was a touch of the Napoleonic. He meant to get into society - and the society he had selected was that of England. Other people have noted the fact - which had impressed itself very firmly on the policeman's mind - that between England and the United States there are three thousand miles of deep water. In the United States, he would be a retired police-captain; in England, an American gentleman of large and independent means with a beautiful daughter.

That was the ruling impulse in his life - his daughter Molly. Though, if he had been a bachelor, he certainly would not have been satisfied to pursue a humble career aloof from graft, on the other hand, if it had not been for Molly, he would not have felt, as he gathered in his dishonest wealth, that he was conducting a sort of holy war. Ever since his wife had died, in his detective-sergeant days, leaving him with a year-old daughter, his ambitions had been inseparably connected with Molly.

All his thoughts were on the future. This New York life was only a preparation for the splendors to come. He spent not a dollar unnecessarily. When Molly was home from school, they lived together simply and quietly in the small house which Molly's taste made so comfortable. The neighbors, knowing his profession and seeing the modest scale on which he lived, told one another that here at any rate was a policeman whose hands were clean of graft. They did not know of the stream that poured week by week and year by year into his bank, to be diverted at intervals into the most profitable channels. Until the time should come for the great change, economy was his motto. The expenses of his home were kept within the bounds of his official salary. All extras went to swell his savings.

He closed his book with a contented sigh, and lighted another cigar. Cigars were his only personal luxury. He drank nothing, ate the simplest food, and made a suit of clothes last for quite an unusual length of time; but no passion for economy could make him deny himself smoke.

He sat on, thinking. It was very late, but he did not feel ready for bed. A great moment had arrived in his affairs. For days, Wall Street had been undergoing one of its periodical fits of jumpiness. There had been rumors and counter-rumors, until finally from the confusion there had soared up like a rocket the one particular stock in which he was most largely interested. He had unloaded that morning, and the result had left him slightly dizzy. The main point to which his mind clung was that the time had come at last. He could make the great change now at any moment that suited him.

He was blowing clouds of smoke and gloating over this fact when the door opened, admitting a bull-terrier, a bull-dog, and in the wake of the procession a girl in a kimono and red slippers.

CHAPTER IV

MOLLY

"Why, Molly," said the policeman, "what are you doing out of bed? I thought you were asleep."

He placed a huge arm around her, and drew her to his lap. As she sat there, his great bulk made her seem smaller than she really was. With her hair down and her little red slippers dangling half a yard from the floor, she seemed a child. McEachern, looking at her, found it hard to realize that nineteen years had passed since the moment when the doctor's raised eyebrows had reproved him for his monosyllabic reception of the news that the baby was a girl.

"Do you know what the time is?" he said. "Two o'clock."

"Much too late for you to be sitting here smoking," said Molly, severely. "How many cigars do you smoke a day? Suppose you had married someone who wouldn't let you smoke!"

"Never stop your husband smoking, my dear. That's a bit of advice for you when you're married."

"I'm never going to marry. I'm going to stop at home,

P.G. Wodehouse

and darn your socks."

"I wish you could," he said, drawing her closer to him. "But one of these days you're going to marry a prince. And now run back to bed. It's much too late - "

"It's no good, father dear. I couldn't get to sleep. I've been trying hard for hours. I've counted sheep till I nearly screamed. It's Rastus' fault. He snores so!"

Mr. McEachern regarded the erring bull-dog sternly.

"Why do you have the brutes in your room?"

"Why, to keep the boogaboos from getting me, of course. Aren't you afraid of the boogaboos getting you? But you're so big, you wouldn't mind. You'd just hit them. And they're not brutes - are you, darlings? You're angels, and you nearly burst yourselves with joy because auntie had come back from England, didn't you? Father, did they miss me when I was gone? Did they pine away?"

"They got like skeletons. We all did."

"You?"

"I should say so."

"Then, why did you send me away to England?"

"I wanted you to see the country. Did you like it?"

"I hated being away from you."

"But you liked the country?"

"I loved it."

McEachern drew a breath of relief. The only possible obstacle to the great change did not exist.

"How would you like to go back to England, Molly?"

"To England! When I've just come home?"

"If I went, too?"

Molly twisted around so that she could see his face better.

"There's something the matter with you, father. You're trying to say something, and I want to know what it is. Tell me quick, or I'll make Rastus bite you!"

"It won't take long, dear. I've been lucky in some investments while you were away, and I'm going to leave the force, and take you over to England, and find a prince for you to marry - if you think you would like it."

"Father! It'll be perfectly splendid!"

"We'll start fair in England, Molly. I'll just be John McEachern, from America, and, if anybody wants to know anything about me, I'm a man who has made money on Wall Street - and that's no lie - and has come over to England to spend it."

Molly gave his arm a squeeze. Her eyes were wet.

"Father, dear," she whispered, "I believe you've been doing it all for me. You've been slaving away for me

P.G. Wodehouse

ever since I was born, stinting yourself and saving money just so that I could have a good time later on."

"No, no!"

"It's true," she said. She turned on him with a tremulous laugh. "I don't believe you've had enough to eat for years. I believe you're all skin and bone. Never mind. To-morrow, I'll take you out and buy you the best dinner you've ever had, out of my own money. We'll go to Sherry's, and you shall start at the top of the menu, and go straight down it till you've had enough."

"That will make up for everything. And, now, don't you think you ought to be going to bed? You'll be losing all that color you got on the ship."

"Soon - not just yet. I haven't seen you for such ages!" She pointed at the bull-terrier. "Look at Tommy, standing there and staring. He can't believe I've really come back. Father, there was a man on the Lusitania with eyes exactly like Tommy's - all brown and bright – and he used to stand and stare just like Tommy's doing."

"If I had been there," said her father wrathfully, "I'd have knocked his head off."

"No, you wouldn't, because I'm sure he was really a very nice young man. He had a chin rather like yours, father. Besides, you couldn't have got at him to knock his head off, because he was traveling second-class."

"Second-class? Then, you didn't talk with him?"

"We couldn't. You wouldn't expect him to shout at me across the railing! Only, whenever I walked round the deck, he seemed to be there."

"Staring!"

"He may not have been staring at me. Probably, he was just looking the way the ship was going, and thinking of some girl in New York. I don't think you can make much of a romance out of it, father."

"I don't want to, my dear. Princes don't travel in the second-cabin."

"He may have been a prince in disguise."

"More likely a drummer," grunted Mr. McEachern.

"Drummers are often quite nice, aren't they?"

"Princes are nicer."

"Well, I'll go to bed and dream of the nicest one I can think of. Come along, dogs. Stop biting my slipper, Tommy. Why can't you behave, like Rastus? Still, you don't snore, do you? Aren't you going to bed soon, father? I believe you've been sitting up late and getting into all sorts of bad habits while I've been away. I'm sure you have been smoking too much. When you've finished that cigar, you're not even to think of another till to-morrow. Promise!"

"Not one?"

"Not one. I'm not going to have my father getting like the people you read about in the magazine advertisements. You don't want to feel sudden shooting pains, do you?"

"No, my dear."

"And have to take some awful medicine?"

"No."

"Then, promise."

"Very well, my dear. I promise."

As the door closed, the captain threw away the stump he was smoking, and remained for a moment in thought. Then, he drew another cigar from his case, lighted it, and resumed the study of the little note-book. It was past three o'clock when he went to his bedroom.

CHAPTER V

A THIEF IN THE NIGHT

How long the light had been darting about the room like a very much enlarged firefly, Jimmy did not know. It seemed to him like hours, for it had woven itself into an incoherent waking dream of his; and for a moment, as the mists of sleep passed away from his brain, he fancied that he was dreaming still. Then, sleep left him, and he realized that the light, which was now moving slowly across the bookcase, was a real light.

That the man behind it could not have been there long was plain, or he would have seen the chair and its occupant. He seemed to be taking the room step by step. As Jimmy sat up noiselessly and gripped the arms of the chair in readiness for a spring, the light passed from the bookcase to the table. Another foot or so to the left, and it would have fallen on Jimmy.

From the position of the ray, Jimmy could see that the burglar was approaching on his side of the table. Though until that day he had not been in the room for two months, its geography was clearly stamped on his mind's eye. He knew almost to a foot where his visitor was standing. Consequently, when, rising swiftly from the chair, he made a football dive into the darkness, it was no speculative dive. It had a conscious aim, and it

P.G. Wodehouse

was not restrained by any uncertainty as to whether the road to the burglar's knees was clear or not.

His shoulder bumped into a human leg. His arms closed instantaneously on it, and pulled. There was a yelp of dismay, and a crash. The lantern bounced away across the room, and wrecked itself on the reef of the steam-heater. Its owner collapsed in a heap on top of Jimmy.

Jimmy, underneath at the fall, speedily put himself uppermost with a twist of his body. He had every advantage. The burglar was a small man, and had been taken very much by surprise, and any fight there might have been in him in normal circumstances had been shaken out of him by the fall. He lay still, not attempting to struggle.

Jimmy half-rose, and, pulling his prisoner by inches to the door, felt up the wall till he found the electric-light button.

The yellow glow that flooded the room disclosed a short, stocky youth of obviously Bowery extraction. A shock of vivid red hair was the first thing about him that caught the eye. A poet would have described it as Titian. Its proprietor's friends and acquaintances probably called it "carrots." Looking up at Jimmy from under this wealth of crimson was a not unpleasing face. It was not handsome, certainly; but there were suggestions of a latent good-humor. The nose had been broken at one period of its career, and one of the ears was undeniably of the cauliflower type; but these are little accidents which may happen to any high-spirited young gentleman. In costume, the visitor had evidently been guided rather by individual taste than by the dictates of fashion. His coat was of rusty black, his trousers of gray, picked out with stains of various colors. Beneath the coat was a faded red-and-white sweater. A hat of soft felt lay on the floor by the table.

The cut of the coat was poor, and the fit of it spoiled by a bulge in one of the pockets. Diagnosing this bulge correctly, Jimmy inserted his hand, and drew out a dingy revolver.

"Well?" he said, rising.

Like most people, he had often wondered what he should do if he were to meet a burglar; and he had always come to the conclusion that curiosity would be his chief emotion. His anticipations were proved perfectly correct. Now that he had abstracted his visitor's gun, he had no wish to do anything but engage him in conversation. A burglar's life was something so entirely outside his experience! He wanted to learn the burglar's point of view. Incidentally, he reflected with amusement, as he recalled his wager, he might pick up a few useful hints.

The man on the floor sat up, and rubbed the back of his head ruefully.

"Gee!" he muttered. "I t'ought some guy had t'rown de buildin' at me."

"It was only little me," said Jimmy. "Sorry if I hurt you at all. You really want a mat for that sort of thing."

The man's hand went furtively to his pocket. Then, his eye caught sight of the revolver, which Jimmy had placed on the table. With a sudden dash, he seized it.

P.G. Wodehouse

"Now, den, boss!" he said, between his teeth.

Jimmy extended his hand, and unclasped it. Six shells lay in the palm.

"Why worry?" he said. "Sit down and let us talk of life."

"It's a fair cop, boss," said the man, resignedly.

"Away with melancholy," said Jimmy. "I'm not going to call the police. You can beat it whenever you like."

The man stared.

"I mean it," said Jimmy. "What's the trouble? I've no grievance. I wish, though, if you haven't any important engagement, you would stop and talk awhile first."

A broad grin spread itself across the other's face. There was something singularly engaging about him when he grinned.

"Gee! If youse ain't goin' to call de cops, I'll talk till de chickens roost ag'in."

"Talking, however," said Jimmy, "is dry work. Are you by any chance on the wagon?"

"What's dat? Me? On your way, boss!"

"Then, you'll find a pretty decent whiskey in that decanter. Help yourself. I think you'll like it."

A musical gurgling, followed by a contented sigh,

showed that the statement had been tested and proved correct.

"Cigar?" asked Jimmy.

"Me fer dat," assented his visitor.

"Take a handful."

"I eats dem alive," said the marauder jovially, gathering in the spoils.

Jimmy crossed his legs.

"By the way," he said, "let there be no secrets between us. What's your name? Mine is Pitt. James Willoughby Pitt."

"Mullins is my monaker, boss. Spike, dey calls me."

"And you make a living at this sort of thing?"

"Not so woise."

"How did you get in here?"

Spike Mullins grinned.

"Gee! Ain't de window open?"

"If it hadn't been?"

"I'd a' busted it."

Jimmy eyed the fellow fixedly.

P.G. Wodehouse

"Can you use an oxy-acetylene blow-pipe?" he demanded.

Spike was on the point of drinking. He lowered his glass, and gaped.

"What's dat?" he said.

"An oxy-acetylene blow-pipe."

"Search me," said Spike, blankly. "Dat gets past me."

Jimmy's manner grew more severe.

"Can you make soup?"

"Soup, boss?"

"He doesn't know what soup is," said Jimmy, despairingly. "My good man, I'm afraid you have missed your vocation. You have no business to be trying to burgle. You don't know the first thing about the game."

Spike was regarding the speaker with disquiet over his glass. Till now, the red-haired one had been very well satisfied with his methods, but criticism was beginning to sap his nerve. He had heard tales of masters of his craft who made use of fearsome implements such as Jimmy had mentioned; burglars who had an airy acquaintanceship, bordering on insolent familiarity, with the marvels of science; men to whom the latest inventions were as familiar as his own jemmy was to himself. Could this be one of that select band? His host began to take on a new aspect in his eyes.

"Spike," said Jimmy.

"Huh?"

"Have you a thorough knowledge of chemistry, physics - "

"On your way, boss!"

" - toxicology - "

"Search me!"

" - electricity and microscopy?"

"... Nine, ten. Dat's de finish. I'm down an' out."

Jimmy shook his head, sadly.

"Give up burglary," he said. "It's not in your line. Better try poultry-farming."

Spike twiddled his glass, abashed.

"Now, I," said Jimmy airily, "am thinking of breaking into a house to-night."

"Gee!" exclaimed Spike, his suspicions confirmed at last. "I t'ought youse was in de game, boss. Sure, you're de guy dat's onto all de curves. I t'ought so all along."

"I should like to hear," said Jimmy amusedly, as one who draws out an intelligent child, "how you would set about burgling one of those up-town villas. My own work has been on a somewhat larger scale and on the other side of the Atlantic."

"De odder side?"

"I have done as much in London, as anywhere else," said Jimmy. "A great town, London, full of opportunities for the fine worker. Did you hear of the cracking of the New Asiatic Bank in Lombard Street?"

"No, boss," whispered Spike. "Was dat you?"

Jimmy laughed.

"The police would like an answer to the same question," he said, self-consciously. "Perhaps, you heard nothing of the disappearance of the Duchess of Havant's diamonds?"

"Wasdat - ?"

"The thief," said Jimmy, flicking a speck of dust from his coat sleeve, "was discovered to have used an oxy-acetylene blow-pipe."

The rapturous intake of Spike's breath was the only sound that broke the silence. Through the smoke, his eyes could be seen slowly widening.

"But about this villa," said Jimmy. "I am always interested even in the humblest sides of the profession. Now, tell me, supposing you were going to break into a villa, what time of night would you do it?"

"I always t'inks it's best either late like dis or when de folks is in at supper," said Spike, respectfully.

Jimmy smiled a faint, patronizing smile, and nodded.

"Well, and what would you do?"

"I'd rubber around some to see isn't dere a window open somewheres," said Spike, diffidently.

"And if there wasn't?"

"I'd climb up de porch an' into one of de bedrooms," said Spike, almost blushing. He felt like a boy reading his first attempts at original poetry to an established critic. What would this master cracksman, this polished wielder of the oxy-acetylene blow-pipe, this expert in toxicology, microscopy and physics think of his callow outpourings!

"How would you get into the bedroom?"

Spike hung his head.

"Bust de catch wit' me jemmy," he whispered, shamefacedly.

"Burst the catch with your jemmy?"

"It's de only way I ever learned," pleaded Spike.

The expert was silent. He seemed to be thinking. The other watched his face, humbly.

"How would youse do it, boss?" he ventured timidly, at last.

"Eh?"

"How would youse do it?"

"Why, I'm not sure," said the master, graciously, "whether your way might not do in a case like that. It's crude, of course, but with a few changes it would do."

"Gee, boss! Is dat right?" queried the astonished disciple.

"It would do," said the master, frowning thoughtfully; "it would do quite well - quite well!"

Spike drew a deep breath of joy and astonishment. That his methods should meet with approval from such a mind...!

"Gee!" he whispered - as who would say, "I and Napoleon."

CHAPTER VI

AN EXHIBITION PERFORMANCE

Cold reason may disapprove of wagers, but without a doubt there is something joyous and lovable in the type of mind that rushes at the least provocation into the making of them, something smacking of the spacious days of the Regency. Nowadays, the spirit seems to have deserted England. When Mr. Asquith became Premier of Great Britain, no earnest forms were to be observed rolling peanuts along the Strand with a toothpick. When Mr. Asquith is dethroned, it is improbable that any Briton will allow his beard to remain unshaved until the Liberal party returns to office. It is in the United States that the wager has found a home. It is characteristic of some minds to dash into a wager with the fearlessness of a soldier in a forlorn hope, and, once in, to regard it almost as a sacred trust. Some men never grow up out of the schoolboy spirit of "daring."

To this class Jimmy Pitt belonged. He was of the same type as the man in the comic opera who proposed to the lady because somebody bet him he wouldn't. There had never been a time when a challenge, a "dare," had not acted as a spur to him. In his newspaper days, life had been one long series of challenges. They had been the essence of the business. A story had not been worth

P.G. Wodehouse

getting unless the getting were difficult.

With the conclusion of his newspaper life came a certain flatness into the scheme of things. There were times, many times, when Jimmy was bored. He hungered for excitement, and life appeared to have so little to offer! The path of the rich man was so smooth, and it seemed to lead nowhere! This task of burgling a house was like an unexpected treat to a child. With an intensity of purpose that should have touched his sense of humor, but, as a matter of fact, did not appeal to him as ludicrous in any way, he addressed himself to the work. The truth was that Jimmy was one of those men who are charged to the, brim with force. Somehow, the force had to find an outlet. If he had undertaken to collect birds' eggs, he would have set about it with the same tense energy.

Spike was sitting on the edge of his chair, dazed but happy, his head still buzzing from the unhoped-for praise. Jimmy looked at his watch. It was nearly three o'clock. A sudden idea struck him. The gods had provided gifts: why not take them?

"Spike!"

"Huh?"

"Would you care to come and crack a crib with me, now?"

Reverential awe was written on the red-haired one's face.

"Gee, boss!"

"Would you?"

"Surest t'ing you know, boss."

"Or, rather," proceeded Jimmy, "would you care to crack a crib while I came along with you? Strictly speaking, I am here on a vacation, but a trifle like this isn't real work. It's this way," he explained. "I've taken a fancy to you, Spike, and I don't like to see you wasting your time on coarse work. You have the root of the matter in you, and with a little coaching I could put a polish on you. I wouldn't do this for everyone, but I hate to see a man bungling who might do better! I want to see you at work. Come right along, and we'll go up-town, and you shall start in. Don't get nervous. Just work as you would if I were not there. I shall not expect too much. Rome was not built in a day. When we are through, I will criticize a few of your mistakes. How does that suit you?"

"Gee, boss! Great! An' I know where dere's a peach of a place, boss. Regular soft proposition. A friend of mine told me. It's - "

"Very well, then. One moment, though."

He went to the telephone. Before he had left New York on his travels, Arthur Mifflin had been living at a hotel near Washington Square. It was probable that he was still there. He called up the number. The night-clerk was an old acquaintance of his.

"Hello, Dixon," said Jimmy, "is that you? I'm Pitt - Pitt! Yes, I'm back. How did you guess? Yes, very pleasant. Has Mr. Mifflin come in yet? Gone to bed? Never mind, call him up, will you? Good."

P.G. Wodehouse

Presently, the sleepy and outraged voice of Mr. Mifflin spoke at the other end of the line.

"What's wrong? Who the devil's that?"

"My dear Arthur! Where you pick up such expressions I can't think - not from me."

"Is that you, Jimmy? What in the name of - !"

"Heavens! What are you kicking about? The night's yet young. Arthur, touching that little arrangement we made - cracking that crib, you know. Are you listening? Have you any objection to my taking an assistant along with me? I don't want to do anything contrary to our agreement, but there's a young fellow here who's anxious that I should let him come along and pick up a few hints. He's a professional all right. Not in our class, of course, but quite a fair rough workman. He - Arthur! Arthur! These are harsh words! Then, am I to understand you have no objection? Very well. Only, don't say later on that I didn't play fair. Good-night."

He hung up the receiver, and turned to Spike.

"Ready?"

"Ain't youse goin' to put on your gum-shoes, boss?"

Jimmy frowned reflectively, as if there was something in what this novice suggested. He went into the bedroom, and returned wearing a pair of thin patent-leather shoes.

Spike coughed tentatively.

"Won't youse need your gun?" he hazarded. Jimmy gave a short laugh.

"I work with brains, not guns," he said. "Let us be going."

There was a taxi-cab near by, as there always is in New York. Jimmy pushed Spike in, and they drove off. To Jimmy, New York stopped somewhere about Seventy-Second Street. Anything beyond that was getting on for the Middle West, and seemed admirably suited as a field for the cracksman. He had a vague idea of up-town as a remote, desolate district, badly lighted - if lighted at all - and sparsely dotted with sleepy policemen.

The luxury of riding in a taxi-cab kept Spike dumb for several miles. Having arrived at what seemed a sufficiently remote part of America, Jimmy paid the driver, who took the money with that magnificently aloof air which characterizes the taxi-chauffeur. A lesser man might have displayed some curiosity about the ill-matched pair. The chauffeur, having lighted a cigarette, drove off without any display of interest whatsoever. It might have been part of his ordinary duties to drive gentlemen in evening clothes and shock-headed youths in parti-colored sweaters about the city at three o'clock in the morning.

"We will now," said Jimmy, "stroll on and prospect. It is up to you, Spike. Didn't you say something about knowing a suitable house somewhere? Are we anywhere near it?"

Spike looked at the number of the street.

"We got some way to go, boss," he said. "I wisht youse hadn't sent away de cab."

"Did you think we were going to drive up to the door? Pull yourself together, my dear man."

They walked on, striking eastward out of Broadway. It caused Jimmy some surprise to find that the much-enduring thoroughfare extended as far as this. It had never occurred to him before to ascertain what Broadway did with itself beyond Times Square.

It was darker now that they had moved from the center of things, but it was still far too light for Jimmy's tastes. He was content, however, to leave matters entirely to his companion. Spike probably had his methods for evading publicity on these occasions.

Spike plodded on. Block after block he passed, until finally the houses began to be more scattered.

At last, he halted before a fair-sized detached house.

"Dis is de place," he said. "A friend of mine tells me of it. I didn't know he was me friend, dough, before he puts me wise about dis joint. I t'ought he'd got it in fer me 'cos of last week when I scrapped wit' him about somet'in'. I t'ought after that he was layin' fer me, but de next time he seen me he put me wise to dis place."

"Coals of fire," said Jimmy. "He was of a forgiving disposition." A single rain-drop descended on the nape of his neck. In another moment, a smart shower had begun.

"This matter has passed out of our hands," said Jimmy.

"We must break in, if only to get shelter. Get busy, my lad."

There was a handy window only a few feet from the ground. Spike pulled from his pocket a small bottle.

"What's that?" inquired Jimmy.

"Molasses, boss," said Spike, deferentially.

He poured the contents of the bottle on a piece of paper, which he pressed firmly against the window-pane. Then, drawing out a short steel instrument, he gave the paper a sharp tap. The glass broke almost inaudibly. The paper came away, leaving a gap in the pane. Spike inserted his hand, shot back the catch, and softly pushed up the window.

"Elementary," said Jimmy; "elementary, but quite neat."

There was now a shutter to be negotiated. This took longer, but in the end Spike's persuasive methods prevailed.

Jimmy became quite cordial.

"You have been well-grounded, Spike," he said. "And, after all, that is half the battle. The advice I give to every novice is, 'Learn to walk before you try to run.' Master the a, b, c, of the craft first. With a little careful coaching, you will do. Just so. Pop in."

Spike climbed cautiously over the sill, followed by Jimmy. The latter struck a match, and found the electric light switch. They were in a parlor, furnished and decorated with surprising taste. Jimmy had expected the usual hideousness, but here everything from the wall-paper to the smallest ornaments was wonderfully well selected.

Business, however, was business. This was no time to stand admiring artistic effects in room-furnishing. There was that big J to be carved on the front door. If 'twere done, then 'twere well 'twere done quickly.

He was just moving to the door, when from some distant part of the house came the bark of a dog. Another joined in. The solo became a duet. The air was filled with their clamor.

"Gee!" cried Spike.

The remark seemed more or less to sum up the situation.

"'Tis sweet," says Byron, "to hear the watch-dog's honest bark." Jimmy and Spike found two watch-dogs' honest barks cloying. Spike intimated this by making a feverish dash for the open window. Unfortunately for the success of this maneuver, the floor of the room was covered not with a carpet but with tastefully scattered rugs, and underneath these rugs it was very highly polished. Spike, treading on one of these islands, was instantly undone. No power of will or muscle can save a man in such a case. Spike skidded. His feet flew from under him. There was a momentary flash of red head, as of a passing meteor. The next moment, he had fallen on his back with a thud that shook the house. Even in the crisis, the thought flashed across Jimmy's mind that this was not Spike's lucky night.

Upstairs, the efforts of the canine choir had begun to resemble the "A che la morte" duet in "Il Trovatore." Particularly good work was being done by the baritone dog.

Spike sat up, groaning. Equipped though he was by nature with a skull of the purest and most solid ivory, the fall had disconcerted him. His eyes, like those of Shakespeare's poet, rolling in a fine frenzy, did glance from heaven to earth, from earth to heaven. He passed his fingers tenderly through his vermilion hair.

Heavy footsteps were descending the stairs. In the distance, the soprano dog had reached A in alt., and was holding it, while his fellow artiste executed runs in the lower register.

"Get up!" hissed Jimmy. "There's somebody coming! Get up, you idiot, can't you!"

It was characteristic of Jimmy that it never even occurred to him to desert the fallen one, and depart alone. Spike was his brother-in-arms. He would as soon have thought of deserting him as a sea-captain would of abandoning the ship.

Consequently, as Spike, despite all exhortations, continued to remain on the floor, rubbing his head and uttering "Gee!" at intervals in a melancholy voice, Jimmy resigned himself to fate, and stood where he was, waiting for the door to open.

It opened the next moment as if a cyclone had been behind it.

CHAPTER VII

GETTING ACQUAINTED

A cyclone, entering a room, is apt to alter the position of things. This cyclone shifted a footstool, a small chair, a rug, and Spike. The chair, struck by a massive boot, whirled against the wall. The foot-stool rolled away. The rug crumpled up and slid. Spike, with a yell, leaped to his feet, slipped again, fell, and finally compromised on an all-fours position, in which attitude he remained, blinking.

While these stirring acts were in progress, there was the sound of a door opening upstairs, followed by a scuttering of feet and an appalling increase in the canine contribution to the current noises. The duet had now taken on quite a Wagnerian effect.

There raced into the room first a white bull-terrier, he of the soprano voice, and - a bad second - his fellow artiste, the baritone, a massive bull-dog, bearing a striking resemblance to the big man with the big lower jaw whose entrance had started the cyclone.

And, then, in theatrical parlance, the entire company "held the picture." Up-stage, with his hand still on the door, stood the man with the jaw; downstage, Jimmy; center, Spike and the bull-dog, their noses a couple of inches apart, inspected each other with mutual disfavor. On the extreme O. P. side, the bull-terrier, who had fallen foul of a wicker-work table, was crouching with extended tongue and rolling eyes, waiting for the next move.

The householder looked at Jimmy. Jimmy looked at the householder. Spike and the bull-dog looked at each other. The bull-terrier distributed his gaze impartially around the company.

"A typical scene of quiet American home-life," murmured Jimmy.

The householder glowered.

"Hands up, you devils!" he roared, pointing a mammoth revolver.

The two marauders humored his whim.

"Let me explain," said Jimmy pacifically, shuffling warily around in order to face the bull-terrier, who was now strolling in his direction with an ill-assumed carelessness.

"Keep still, you blackguard!"

Jimmy kept still. The bull-terrier, with the same abstracted air, was beginning a casual inspection of his right trouser-leg.

Relations between Spike and the bull-dog, meanwhile, had become more strained. The sudden flinging up of the former's arms had had the worst effects on the animal's nerves. Spike, the croucher on all-fours, he might have tolerated; but Spike, the semaphore, inspired him with thoughts of battle. He was growling in a moody, reflective manner. His eye was full of purpose.

It was probably this that caused Spike to look at the householder. Till then, he had been too busy to shift his gaze, but now the bull-dog's eye had become so unpleasing that he cast a pathetic glance up at the man by the door.

"Gee!" he cried. "It's de boss. Say, boss, call off de dawg. It's sure goin' to nip de hull head off'n me."

The other lowered the revolver in surprise.

"So, it's you, you limb of Satan!" he remarked. "I thought I had seen that damned red head of yours before. What are you doing in my house?"

Spike uttered a howl in which indignation and self-pity were nicely blended.

"I'll lay for that Swede!" he cried. "I'll soak it to him good! Boss, I've had a raw deal. On de level, I has. Dey's a feller I know, a fat Swede - Ole Larsen his monaker is - an' dis feller an' me started in scrapping last week, an' I puts it all over him, so he had it in for me. But he comes up to me, like as if he's meanin' to be good, an' he says he's got a soft proposition fer me if I'll give him half. So, I says all right, where is it? An' he gives me de number of dis house, an' says dis is where a widder-lady lives all alone, an' has got silver mugs and t'ings to boin, an' dat she's away down Sout', so dere ain't nobody in de house. Gee! I'll soak it to dat Swede! It was a raw deal, boss. He was just hopin' to put me in bad wit' you. Dat's how it was, boss. Honest!"

The big man listened to this sad story of Grecian gifts in silence. Not so the bull-dog, which growled from start to finish.

Spike eyed it uneasily.

"Won't you call off de dawg, boss?" he said.

The other stooped, and grasped the animal's collar, jerking him away.

"The same treatment," suggested Jimmy with approval, "would also do a world of good to this playful and affectionate animal - unless he is a vegetarian. In which case, don't bother."

The big man glowered at him.

"Who are you?" he demanded.

"My name," began Jimmy, "is - "

"Say," said Spike, "he's a champion burglar, boss - "

The householder shut the door.

"Eh?" he said.

"He's a champion burglar from de odder side. He sure is. From Lunnon. Gee, he's de guy! Tell him about de bank you opened, an' de jools you swiped from de duchess, an' de what-d'ye-call-it blow-pipe."

It seemed to Jimmy that Spike was showing a certain want of tact. When you are discovered by a householder - with revolver - in his parlor at half-past three in the morning, it is surely an injudicious move to lay stress on your proficiency as a burglar. The householder may be supposed to take that for granted. The side of your character that should be advertised in such a crisis is the non-burglarious. Allusion should be made to the fact that, as a child, you attended Sunday school regularly, and to what the minister said when you took the divinity prize. The idea should be conveyed to the householder's mind that, if let off with a caution, your innate goodness of heart will lead you to reform and to avoid such scenes in future.

With some astonishment, therefore, Jimmy found that these revelations, so far from prejudicing the man with the revolver against him, had apparently told in his favor. The man behind the gun was regarding him rather with interest than disapproval.

"So, you're a crook from London, are you?"

Jimmy did not hesitate. If being a crook from London was a passport into citizens' parlors in the small hours, and, more particularly, if it carried with it also a safe-conduct out of them, Jimmy was not the man to refuse the role. He bowed.

"Well, you'll have to come across, now you're in New York. Understand that! And come across good."

"Sure, he will," said Spike, charmed that the tension had been relieved, and matters placed upon a pleasant and business-like footing. "He'll be good. He's next to de game, sure."

"Sure," echoed Jimmy, courteously. He did not understand; but things seemed to be taking a turn for the better, so why disturb the harmony?

"Dis gent," said Spike respectfully, "is boss of de cops. A police-captain," he corrected himself.

A light broke upon Jimmy's darkness. He wondered he had not understood before. He had not been a newspaper-man in New York for a year without finding out something of the inner workings of the police force. He saw now why the other's manner had changed.

"Pleased to meet you," he said. "We must have a talk together one of these days."

"We must," said the police-captain, significantly. He was rich, richer than he had ever hoped to be; but he was still on Tom Tiddler's ground, and meant to make the most of it.

"Of course, I don't know your methods on this side, but anything that's usual - "

"I'll see you at my office. Spike Mullins will show you where it is."

"Very well. You must forgive this preliminary informal call. We came in more to shelter from the rain than anything."

"You did, did you?"

Jimmy felt that it behooved him to stand on his dignity. The situation demanded it.

"Why," he said with some hauteur, "in the ordinary course of business I should hardly waste time over a small crib like - "

"It's banks fer his," murmured Spike, rapturously. "He eats dem alive. An' jools from duchesses."

"I admit a partiality for jewels and duchesses," said Jimmy. "And, now, as it's a little late, perhaps we had better - Ready, Spike? Good-night, then. Pleased to have met you."

"I'll see you at my office."

"I may possibly look in. I shall be doing very little work in New York, I fancy. I am here merely on a vacation."

"If you do any work at all," said the policeman coldly, "you'll look in at my office, or you'll wish you had when it's too late."

"Of course, of course. I shouldn't dream of omitting any formality that may be usual. But I don't fancy I shall break my vacation. By the way, one little thing. Have you. any objections to my carving a J on your front-door?"

The policeman stared.

"On the inside. It won't show. It's just a whim of mine. If you have no objection?"

"I don't want any of your - " began the policeman.

"You misunderstand me. It's only that it means paying

for a dinner. I wouldn't for the world - "

The policeman pointed to the window.

"Out you get," he said, abruptly. "I've had enough of you. And don't you forget to come to my office."

Spike, still deeply mistrustful of the bull-dog Rastus, jumped at the invitation. He was through the window and out of sight in the friendly darkness almost before the policeman had finished speaking. Jimmy remained.

"I shall be delighted - " he had begun. Then, he stopped. In the doorway was standing a girl - a girl whom he recognized. Her startled look told him that she, too, had recognized him.

Not for the first time since he had set out from his flat that night in Spike's company, Jimmy was conscious of a sense of the unreality of things. It was all so exactly as it would have happened in a dream! He had gone to sleep thinking of this girl, and here she was. But a glance at the man with the revolver brought him back to earth. There was nothing of the dream-world about the police-captain.

That gentleman, whose back was toward the door, had not observed the addition to the company. Molly had turned the handle quietly, and her slippered feet made no sound. It was the amazed expression on Jimmy's face that caused the captain to look toward the door.

"Molly!"

The girl smiled, though her face was white. Jimmy's evening clothes had reassured her. She did not understand how he came to be there, but evidently there was nothing wrong. She had interrupted a conversation, not a conflict.

"I heard the noise and you going downstairs, and I sent the dogs down to help you, father," she said. "And, then, after a little, I came down to see if you were all right."

Mr. McEachern was perplexed. Molly's arrival had put him in an awkward position. To denounce the visitor as a cracksman was now impossible, for he knew too much. The only real fear of the policeman's life was lest some word of his money-making methods might come to his daughter's ears.

Quite a brilliant idea came to him.

"A man broke in, my dear," he said. "This gentleman was passing, and saw him."

"Distinctly," said Jimmy. "An ugly-looking customer!"

"But he slipped out of the window, and got away," concluded the policeman.

"He was very quick," said Jimmy. "I think he may have been a professional acrobat."

"He didn't hurt you, father?"

"No, no, my dear."

"Perhaps I frightened him," said Jimmy, airily.

Mr. McEachern scowled furtively at him.

"We mustn't detain you, Mr.-"

"Pitt," said Jimmy. "My name is Pitt." He turned to Molly. "I hope you enjoyed the voyage."

The policeman started.

"You know my daughter?"

"By sight only, I'm afraid. We were fellow-passengers on the Lusitania. Unfortunately, I was in the second-cabin. I used to see your daughter walking the deck sometimes."

Molly smiled.

"I remember seeing you - sometimes."

McEachern burst out.

"Then, you - !"

He stopped, and looked at Molly. The girl was bending over Rastus, tickling him under the ear.

"Let me show you the way out, Mr. Pitt," said the policeman, shortly. His manner was abrupt, but when one is speaking to a man whom one would dearly love to throw out of the window, abruptness is almost unavoidable.

"Perhaps I should be going," said Jimmy.

"Good-night, Mr. Pitt," said Molly.

"I hope we shall meet again," said Jimmy.

"This way, Mr. Pitt," growled McEachern, holding the door.

"Please don't trouble," said Jimmy. He went to the window, and, flinging his leg over the sill, dropped noiselessly to the ground.

He turned and put his head in at the window again.

"I did that rather well," he said, pleasantly. "I think I must take up this - sort of thing as a profession. Good-night."

CHAPTER VIII

AT DREEVER

In the days before he began to expend his surplus energy in playing Rugby football, the Welshman was accustomed, whenever the monotony of his everyday life began to oppress him, to collect a few friends and make raids across the border into England, to the huge discomfort of the dwellers on the other side. It was to cope with this habit that Dreever Castle, in the county of Shropshire, came into existence. It met a long-felt want. In time of trouble, it became a haven of refuge. From all sides, people poured into it, emerging cautiously when the marauders had disappeared. In the whole history of the castle, there is but one instance recorded of a bandit attempting to take the place by storm, and the attack was an emphatic failure. On receipt of a ladleful of molten lead, aimed to a nicety by one John, the Chaplain (evidently one of those sporting parsons), this warrior retired, done to a turn, to his mountain fastnesses, and was never heard of again. He would seem, however, to have passed the word around among his friends, for subsequent raiding parties studiously avoided the castle, and a peasant who had succeeded in crossing its threshold was for the future considered to he "home" and out of the game.

P.G. Wodehouse

Such was the Dreever of old. In later days, the Welshman having calmed down considerably, it had lost its militant character. The old walls still stood, gray, menacing and unchanged, hut they were the only link with the past. The castle was now a very comfortable country-house, nominally ruled over by Hildebrand Spencer Poynt de Burgh John Hannasyde Coombe-Crombie, twelfth Earl of Dreever ("Spennie" to his relatives and intimates), a light-haired young gentleman of twenty-four, but in reality the possession of his uncle and aunt, Sir Thomas and Lady Julia Blunt.

Lord Dreever's position was one of some embarrassment. At no point in their history had the Dreevers been what one might call a parsimonious family. If a chance presented itself of losing money in a particularly wild and futile manner, the Dreever of the period had invariably sprung at it with the vim of an energetic blood-hound. The South Sea Bubble absorbed two hundred thousand pounds of good Dreever money, and the remainder of the family fortune was squandered to the ultimate penny by the sportive gentleman who held the title in the days of the Regency, when Watier's and the Cocoa Tree were in their prime, and fortunes had a habit of disappearing in a single evening. When Spennie became Earl of Dreever, there was about one dollar and thirty cents in the family coffers.

This is the point at which Sir Thomas Blunt breaks into Dreever history. Sir Thomas was a small, pink, fussy, obstinate man with a genius for trade and the ambition of an Alexander the Great; probably one of the finest and most complete specimens of the came-over-Waterloo-Bridge-with-half-a crown-in-my-pocket-and

-now-look-at-me class of millionaires in existence. He had started almost literally with nothing. By carefully excluding from his mind every thought except that of making money, he had risen in the world with a gruesome persistence which nothing could check. At the age of fifty-one, he was chairman of Blunt's Stores, L't'd, a member of Parliament (silent as a wax figure, but a great comfort to the party by virtue of liberal contributions to its funds), and a knight. This was good, but he aimed still higher; and, meeting Spennie's aunt, Lady Julia Coombe-Crombie, just at the moment when, financially, the Dreevers were at their lowest ebb, he had effected a very satisfactory deal by marrying her, thereby becoming, as one might say, Chairman of Dreever, L't'd. Until Spennie should marry money, an act on which his chairman vehemently insisted, Sir Thomas held the purse, and except in minor matters ordered by his wife, of whom he stood in uneasy awe, had things entirely his own way.

One afternoon, a little over a year after the events recorded in the preceding chapter, Sir Thomas was in his private room, looking out of the window, from which the view was very beautiful. The castle stood on a hill, the lower portion of which, between the house and the lake, had been cut into broad terraces. The lake itself and its island with the little boat-house in the center gave a glimpse of fairyland.

But it was not altogether the beauty of the view that had drawn Sir Thomas to the window. He was looking at it chiefly because the position enabled him to avoid his wife's eye; and just at the moment be was rather anxious to avoid his wife's eye. A somewhat stormy board-meeting was in progress, and Lady Julia, who

P.G. Wodehouse

constituted the board of directors, had been heckling the chairman. The point under discussion was one of etiquette, and in matters of etiquette Sir Thomas felt himself at a disadvantage.

"I tell you, my dear," he said to the window, "I am not easy in my mind."

"Nonsense," snapped Lady Julia; "absurd - ridiculous!"

Lady Julia Blunt, when conversing, resembled a Maxim gun more than anything else.

"But your diamonds, my dear."

"We can take care of them."

"But why should we have the trouble? Now, if we - "

"It's no trouble."

"When we were married, there was a detective - "

"Don't be childish, Thomas. Detectives at weddings are quite customary."

"But - "

"Bah!"

"I paid twenty thousand pounds for that rope of diamonds," said Sir Thomas, obstinately. Switch things upon a cash basis, and he was more at ease.

"May I ask if you suspect any of our guests of being

criminals?" inquired Lady Julia, with a glance of chill disdain.

Sir Thomas looked out of the window. At the moment, the sternest censor could have found nothing to cavil at in the movements of such of the house-party as were in sight. Some were playing tennis, some clock-golf, and others were smoking.

"Why, no," he admitted.

"Of course. Absurd - quite absurd!"

"But the servants. We have engaged a number of new servants lately."

"With excellent recommendations."

Sir Thomas was on the point of suggesting that the recommendations might be forged, but his courage failed him. Julia was sometimes so abrupt in these little discussions! She did not enter into his point of view. He was always a trifle inclined to treat the castle as a branch of Blunt's Stores. As proprietor of the stores, he had made a point of suspecting everybody, and the results had been excellent. In Blunt's Stores, you could hardly move in any direction without bumping into a gentlemanly detective, efficiently disguised. For the life of him, Sir Thomas could not see why the same principle should not obtain at Dreever. Guests at a country house do not as a rule steal their host's possessions, but then it is only an occasional customer at a store who goes in for shop-lifting. It was the principle of the thing, he thought: Be prepared against every emergency. With Sir Thomas Blunt, suspiciousness was almost a mania. He was forced to admit that the chances were against any of his guests exhibiting larcenous tendencies, but, as for the servants, he thoroughly mistrusted them all, except Saunders, the butler. It had seemed to him the merest prudence that a detective from a private inquiry agency should be installed at the castle while the house was full. Somewhat rashly, he had mentioned this to his wife, and Lady Julia's critique of the scheme had been terse and unflattering.

"I suppose," said Lady Julia sarcastically, "you will jump to the conclusion that this man whom Spennie is bringing down with him to-day is a criminal of some sort?"

"Eh? Is Spennie bringing a friend?"

There was not a great deal of enthusiasm in Sir Thomas's voice. His nephew was not a young man whom he respected very highly. Spennie regarded his uncle with nervous apprehension, as one who would deal with his short-comings with vigor and severity. Sir Thomas, for his part, looked on Spennie as a youth who would get into mischief unless under his uncle's eye.

"I had a telegram from him just now," Lady Julia explained.

"Who is his friend?"

"He doesn't say. He just says he's a man he met in London."

"H'm!"

"And what does, 'H'm!' mean?" demanded Lady Julia.

"A man can pick up strange people in London," said Sir Thomas, judicially.

"Nonsense!"

"Just as you say, my dear."

Lady Julia rose.

"As for what you suggest about the detective, it is of course absolutely absurd."

"Quite so, my dear."

"You mustn't think of it."

"Just as you say, my dear."

Lady Julia left the room.

What followed may afford some slight clue to the secret of Sir Thomas Blunt's rise in the world. It certainly suggests singleness of purpose, which is one of the essentials of success.

No sooner had the door closed behind Lady Julia than he went to his writing-table, took pen and paper, and wrote the following letter:

To the Manager,
Wragge's Detective Agency. Holborn Bars,
London E. C.

SIR: With reference to my last of the 28th, ult., I

should be glad if you would send down immediately one of your best men. Am making arrangements to receive him. Kindly instruct him to present himself at Dreever Castle as applicant for position of valet to myself. I will see and engage him on his arrival, and further instruct him in his duties.

Yours faithfully,

THOS. BLUNT.

P. S. I shall expect him to-morrow evening. There is a good train leaving Paddington at 2:15.

Sir Thomas read this over, put in a comma, then placed it in an envelope, and lighted a cigar with the air of one who can be checked, yes, but vanquished, never.

CHAPTER IX

FRIENDS, NEW AND OLD

On the night of the day on which Sir Thomas Blunt wrote and dispatched his letter to Wragge's Detective Agency, Jimmy Pitt chanced to stop at the Savoy.

If you have the money and the clothes, and do not object to being turned out into the night just as you are beginning to enjoy yourself, there are few things pleasanter than supper at the Savoy Hotel, London. But, as Jimmy sat there, eying the multitude through the smoke of his cigarette, he felt, despite all the brightness and glitter, that this was a flat world, and that he was very much alone in it.

A little over a year had passed since the merry evening at Police-Captain McEachern's. During that time, he had covered a good deal of new ground. His restlessness had reasserted itself. Somebody had mentioned Morocco in his hearing, and a fortnight later he was in Fez.

Of the principals in that night's drama, he had seen nothing more. It was only when, after walking home on air, rejoicing over the strange chance that had led to his finding and having speech with the lady of the Lusitania, he had reached Fifty-Ninth Street, that he realized how he had also lost her. It suddenly came home to him that not only did he not know her address, but he was ignorant of her name. Spike had called the man with the revolver "boss" throughout - only that and nothing more. Except that he was a police-captain, Jimmy knew as little about the man as he had before their meeting. And Spike, who held the key to the mystery, had vanished. His acquaintances of that night had passed out of his life like figures in a waking dream. As far as the big man with the pistol was concerned, this did not distress him. He had known that massive person only for about a quarter of an hour, but to his thinking that was ample. Spike he would have liked to meet again, but he bore the separation with much fortitude. There remained the girl of the ship; and she had haunted him with unfailing persistence during every one of the three hundred and eighty-four days that had passed since their meeting.

It was the thought of her that had made New York seem cramped. For weeks, Jimmy had patrolled the likely streets, the Park, and Riverside Drive, in the hope of meeting her. He had gone to the theaters and restaurants, but with no success. Sometimes, he had wandered through the Bowery, on the chance of meeting Spike. He had seen red heads in profusion, but never again that of his young disciple in the art of burglary. In the end, he had wearied of the other friends of the Strollers, had gone out again on his wanderings. He was greatly missed, especially by that large section of his circle which was in a perpetual state of wanting a little to see it through till Saturday. For years, Jimmy had been to these unfortunates a human bank on which they could draw at will. It offended them that one of those rare natures which are always good for two dollars at any hour of the day should be allowed to waste itself on places like

Morocco and Spain - especially Morocco, where, by all accounts, there were brigands with almost a New York sense of touch.

They argued earnestly with Jimmy. They spoke of Raisuli and Kaid MacLean. But Jimmy was not to be stopped. The gad-fly was vexing him, and he had to move.

For a year, he had wandered, realizing every day the truth of Horace's philosophy for those who travel, that a man cannot change his feelings with his climate, until finally he had found himself, as every wanderer does, at Charing Cross.

At this point, he had tried to rally. Such running away, he told himself, was futile. He would stand still and fight the fever in him.

He had been fighting it now for a matter of two weeks, and already he was contemplating retreat. A man at luncheon had been talking about Japan -

Watching the crowd, Jimmy had found his attention attracted chiefly by a party of three, a few tables away. The party consisted of a girl, rather pretty, a lady of middle age and stately demeanor, plainly her mother, and a light-haired, weedy young man in the twenties. It had been the almost incessant prattle of this youth and the peculiarly high-pitched, gurgling laugh which shot from him at short intervals that had drawn Jimmy's notice upon them. And it was the curious cessation of both prattle and laugh that now made him look again in their direction.

The young man faced Jimmy; and Jimmy, looking at

him, could see that all was not well with him. He was pale. He talked at random. A slight perspiration was noticeable on his forhead.

Jimmy caught his eye. There was a hunted look in it.

Given the time and the place, there were only two things that could have caused this look. Either the light-haired young man had seen a ghost, or he had suddenly realized that he had not enough money to pay the check.

Jimmy's heart went out to the sufferer. He took a card from his case, scribbled the words, "Can I help?" on it, and gave it to a waiter to take to the young man, who was now in a state bordering on collapse.

The next moment, the light-haired one was at his table, talking in a feverish whisper.

"I say," he said, "it's frightfully good of you, old chap! It's frightfully awkward. I've come out with too little money. I hardly like to - you've never seen me before - "

"Don't rub in my misfortunes," pleaded Jimmy. "It wasn't my fault."

He placed a five-pound note on the table.

"Say when," he said, producing another.

"I say, thanks fearfully," the young man said. "I don't know what I'd have done." He grabbed at the note. "I'll let you have it back to-morrow. Here's my card. Is your address on your card? I can't remember. Oh, by Jove,

I've got it in my hand all the time." The gurgling laugh came into action again, freshened and strengthened by its rest. "Savoy Mansions, eh? I'll come round tomorrow. Thanks frightfully again, old chap. I don't know what I should have done."

"It's been a treat," said Jimmy, deprecatingly.

The young man flitted back to his table, bearing the spoil. Jimmy looked at the card he had left. "Lord Dreever," it read, and in the corner the name of a well-known club. The name Dreever was familiar to Jimmy. Everyone knew of Dreever Castle, partly because it was one of the oldest houses in England, but principally because for centuries it had been advertised by a particularly gruesome ghost-story. Everyone had heard of the secret of Dreever, which was known only to the earl and the family lawyer, and confided to the heir at midnight on his twenty-first birthday. Jimmy had come across the story in corners of the papers all over the States, from New York to Onehorseville, Iowa. He looked with interest at the light-haired young man, the latest depository of the awful secret. It was popularly supposed that the heir, after hearing it, never smiled again; but it did not seem to have affected the present Lord Dreever to any great extent. His gurgling laugh was drowning the orchestra. Probably, Jimmy thought, when the family lawyer had told the light-haired young man the secret, the latter's comment had been, "No, really? By Jove, I say, you know!"

Jimmy paid his bill, and got up to go.

It was a perfect summer night - too perfect for bed. Jimmy strolled on to the Embankment, and stood leaning over the balustrade, looking across the river at the vague, mysterious mass of buildings on the Surrey side.

He must have been standing there for some time, his thoughts far away, when a voice spoke at his elbow.

"I say. Excuse me, have you - Hullo!" It was his light-haired lordship of Dreever. "I say, by Jove, why we're always meeting!"

A tramp on a bench close by stirred uneasily in his sleep as the gurgling laugh rippled the air.

"Been looking at the water?" inquired Lord Dreever. "I have. I often do. Don't you think it sort of makes a chap feel - oh, you know. Sort of - I don't know how to put it."

"Mushy?" said Jimmy.

"I was going to say poetical. Suppose there's a girl - "

He paused, and looked down at the water. Jimmy was sympathetic with this mood of contemplation, for in his case, too, there was a girl.

"I saw my party off in a taxi," continued Lord Dreever, "and came down here for a smoke; only, I hadn't a match. Have you - ?"

Jimmy handed over his match-box. Lord Dreever lighted a cigar, and fixed his gaze once more on the river.

"Ripping it looks," he said.

Jimmy nodded.

"Funny thing," said Lord Dreever. "In the daytime, the water here looks all muddy and beastly. Damn' depressing, I call it. But at night - " He paused. "I say," he went on after a moment, "Did you see the girl I was with at the Savoy?"

"Yes," said Jimmy.

"She's a ripper," said Lord Dreever, devoutly.

On the Thames Embankment, in the small hours of a summer morning, there is no such thing as a stranger. The man you talk with is a friend, and, if he will listen - as, by the etiquette of the place, he must - you may pour out your heart to him without restraint. It is expected of you!

"I'm fearfully in love with her," said his lordship.

"She looked a charming girl," said Jimmy.

They examined the water in silence. From somewhere out in the night came the sound of oars, as the police-boat moved on its patrol.

"Does she make you want to go to Japan?" asked Jimmy, suddenly.

"Eh?" said Lord Dreever, startled. "Japan?"

Jimmy adroitly abandoned the position of confidant, and seized that of confider.

"I met a girl a year ago - only really met her once, and

P.G. Wodehouse

even then - oh, well! Anyway, it's made me so restless that I haven't been able to stay in one place for more than a month on end. I tried Morocco, and had to quit. I tried Spain, and that wasn't any good, either. The other day, I heard a fellow say that Japan was a pretty interesting sort of country. I was wondering whether I wouldn't give it a trial."

Lord Dreever regarded this traveled man with interest.

"It beats me," he said, wonderingly. "What do you want to leg it about the world like that for? What's the trouble? Why don't you stay where the girl is?"

"I don't know where she is."

"Don't know?"

"She disappeared."

"Where did you see her last?" asked his lordship, as if Molly were a mislaid penknife.

"New York."

"But how do you mean, disappeared? Don't you know her address?"

"I don't even know her name."

"But dash it all, I say, I mean! Have you ever spoken to her?"

"Only once. It's rather a complicated story. At any rate, she's gone."

Lord Dreever said that it was a rum business. Jimmy conceded the point.

"Seems to me," said his lordship, "we're both in the cart."

"What's your trouble?"

Lord Dreever hesitated.

"Oh, well, it's only that I want to marry one girl, and my uncle's dead set on my marrying another."

"Are you afraid of hurting your uncle's feelings?"

"It's not so much hurting his feelings. It's - oh, well, it's too long to tell now. I think I'll be getting home. I'm staying at our place in Eaton Square."

"How are you going? If you'll walk, I'll come some of the way with you."

"Right you are. Let's be pushing along, shall we?"

They turned up into the Strand, and through Trafalgar Square into Piccadilly. Piccadilly has a restful aspect in the small hours. Some men were cleaning the road with water from a long hose. The swishing of the torrent on the parched wood was musical.

Just beyond the gate of Hyde Park, to the right of the road, stands a cabmen's shelter. Conversation and emotion had made Lord Dreever thirsty. He suggested coffee as a suitable conclusion to the night's revels.

"I often go in here when I'm up in town," he said. "The

P.G. Wodehouse

cabbies don't mind. They're sportsmen."

The shelter was nearly full when they opened the door. It was very warm inside. A cabman gets so much fresh air in the exercise of his professional duties that he is apt to avoid it in private life. The air was heavy with conflicting scents. Fried onions seemed to be having the best of the struggle for the moment, though plug tobacco competed gallantly. A keenly analytical nose might also have detected the presence of steak and coffee.

A dispute seemed to be in progress as they entered.

"You don't wish you was in Russher," said a voice.

"Yus, I do wish I wos in Russher," retorted a shriveled mummy of a cabman, who was blowing patiently at a saucerful of coffee.

"Why do you wish you was in Russher?" asked the interlocutor, introducing a Massa Bones and Massa Johnsing touch into the dialogue.

"Because yer can wade over yer knees in bla-a-a-ad there," said the mummy.

"In wot?"

"In bla-a-ad - ruddy bla-a-ad! That's why I wish I wos in Russher."

"Cheery cove that," said Lord Dreever. "I say, can you give us some coffee?"

"I might try Russia instead of Japan," said

Jimmy, meditatively.

The lethal liquid was brought. Conversation began again. Other experts gave their views on the internal affairs of Russia. Jimmy would have enjoyed it more if he had been less sleepy. His back was wedged comfortably against the wall of the shelter, and the heat of the room stole into his brain. The voices of the disputants grew fainter and fainter.

He had almost dozed off when a new voice cut through the murmur and woke him. It was a voice he knew, and the accent was a familiar accent.

"Gents! Excuse me."

He looked up. The mists of sleep shredded away. A ragged youth with a crop of fiery red hair was standing in the doorway, regarding the occupants of the shelter with a grin, half-whimsical, half-defiant.

Jimmy recognized him. It was Spike Mullins.

"Excuse me," said Spike Mullins. "Is dere any gent in dis bunch of professional beauts wants to give a poor orphan dat suffers from a painful toist something to drink? Gents is courteously requested not to speak all in a crowd."

"Shet that blanky door," said the mummy cabman, sourly.

"And 'op it," added his late opponent. "We don't want none of your sort 'ere."

"Den you ain't my long-lost brudders after all," said the

newcomer, regretfully. "I t'ought youse didn't look handsome enough for dat. Good-night to youse, gents."

"Shet that door, can't yer, when I'm telling yer!" said the mummy, with increased asperity.

Spike was reluctantly withdrawing, when Jimmy rose.

"One moment," he said.

Never in his life had Jimmy failed to stand by a friend in need. Spike was not, perhaps, exactly a friend, but even an acquaintance could rely on Jimmy when down in the world. And Spike was manifestly in that condition.

A look of surprise came into the Bowery Boy's face, followed by one of stolid woodenness. He took the sovereign that Jimmy held out to him with a muttered word of thanks, and shuffled out of the room.

"Can't see what you wanted to give him anything for," said Lord Dreever. "Chap'll only spend it getting soused."

"Oh, he reminded me of a man I used to know."

"Did he? Barnum's what-is-it, I should think," said his lordship. "Shall we be moving?"

CHAPTER X

JIMMY ADOPTS A LAME DOG

A black figure detached itself from the blacker shadows, and shuffled stealthily to where Jimmy stood on the doorstep.

"That you, Spike?" asked Jimmy.

"Dat's right, boss."

"Come on in."

He led the way up to his rooms, switched on the electric light, and shut the door. Spike stood blinking at the sudden glare. He twirled his battered hat in his hands. His red hair shone fiercely.

Jimmy inspected him out of the corner of his eye, and came to the conclusion that the Mullins finances must be at a low ebb. Spike's costume differed in several important details from that of the ordinary well-groomed man about town. There was nothing of the flaneur about the Bowery Boy. His hat was of the soft black felt fashionable on the East Side of New York. It was in poor condition, and looked as if it had been up too late the night before. A black tail-coat, burst at the elbows and stained with mud, was tightly buttoned

P.G. Wodehouse

across his chest, this evidently with the idea of concealing the fact that he wore no shirt - an attempt which was not wholly successful. A pair of gray flannel trousers and boots out of which two toes peeped coyly completed the picture.

Even Spike himself seemed to be aware that there were points in his appearance which would have distressed the editor of a men's fashion-paper.

"'Scuse these duds," he said. "Me man's bin an' mislaid de trunk wit' me best suit in. Dis is me number two."

"Don't mention it, Spike," said Jimmy. "You look a perfect matinee idol. Have a drink?"

Spike's eyes gleamed as he reached for the decanter. He took a seat.

"Cigar, Spike?"

"Sure. T'anks, boss."

Jimmy lighted his pipe. Spike, after a few genteel sips, threw off his restraint, and finished the rest of his glass at a gulp.

"Try another," suggested Jimmy.

Spike's grin showed that the idea had been well received.

Jimmy sat and smoked in silence for a while. He was thinking the thing over. He felt like a detective who has found a clue. At last, he would be able to discover the name of the Lusitania girl. The discovery would not take him very far certainly, but it would be something. Possibly, Spike might even be able to fix the position of the house they had broken into that night.

Spike was looking at Jimmy over his glass in silent admiration. This flat which Jimmy had rented for a year, in the hope that the possession of a fixed abode might help to tie him down to one spot, was handsomely, even luxuriously, furnished. To Spike, every chair and table in the room had a romance of its own, as having been purchased out of the proceeds of that New Asiatic Bank robbery, or from the revenue accruing from the Duchess of Havant's jewels. He was dumb with reverence for one who could make burglary pay to this extent. In his own case, the profession had rarely provided anything more than bread and butter, and an occasional trip to Coney Island.

Jimmy caught his eye, and spoke.

"Well, Spike," he said. "Curious that we should meet like this?"

"De limit," agreed Spike.

"I can't imagine you three thousand miles from New York. How do you know the cars still run both ways on Broadway?"

A wistful look came into Spike's eyes.

"I've been dis side t'ree months. I t'ought it was time I give old Lunnon a call. T'ings was gettin' too fierce in Noo York. De cops was layin' fer me. Dey didn't seem like as if they had any use fer me. So, I beat it."

P.G. Wodehouse

"Bad luck," said Jimmy.

"Fierce," agreed Spike.

"Say, Spike," said Jimmy, "do you know, I spent a whole heap of time before I left New York looking for you?"

"Gee! I wish you'd found me! Did youse want me to help on some lay, boss? Is it a bank, or - jools?"

"Well, no, not that. Do you remember that night we broke into that house uptown - the police-captain's house?"

"Sure."

"What was his name?"

"What, de cop's? Why, McEachern, boss."

"McWhat? How do you spell it?"

"Search me," said Spike, simply.

"Say it again. Fill your lungs, and enunciate slowly and clearly. Be bell-like. Now."

"McEachern."

"Ah! And where was the house? Can you remember that?"

Spike's forehead wrinkled.

"It's gone," he said, at last. "It was somewheres up

some street up de town."

"That's a lot of help," said Jimmy. "Try again."

"It'll come back some time, boss, sure."

"Then, I'm going to keep an eye on you till it does. Just for the moment, you're the most important man in the world to me. Where are you living?"

"Me! Why, in de Park. Dat's right. One of dem swell detached benches wit' a Southern exposure."

"Well, unless you prefer it, you needn't sleep in the Park any more. You can pitch your moving tent with me."

"What, here, boss?"

"Unless we move."

"Me fer dis," said Spike, rolling luxuriously in his chair.

"You'll want some clothes," said Jimmy. "We'll get those to-morrow. You're the sort of figure they can fit off the peg. You're not too tall, which is a good thing."

"Bad t'ing fer me, boss. If I'd been taller, I'd have stood fer being a cop, an' bin buyin' a brownstone house on Fifth Avenue by dis. It's de cops makes de big money in little old Manhattan, dat's who it is."

"The man who knows!" said Jimmy. "Tell me more, Spike. I suppose a good many of the New York force do get rich by graft?"

P.G. Wodehouse

"Sure. Look at old man McEachern."

"I wish I could. Tell me about him, Spike. You seemed to know him pretty well."

"Me? Sure. Dere wasn't a woise old grafter dan him in de bunch. He was out fer de dough all de time. But, say, did youse ever see his girl?"

"What's that?" said Jimmy, sharply.

"I seen her once." Spike became almost lyrical in his enthusiasm. "Gee! She was a boid - a peach fer fair. I'd have left me happy home fer her. Molly was her monaker. She - "

Jimmy was glaring at him.

"Cut it out!" he cried.

"What's dat, boss?" said Spike.

"Cut it out!" said Jimmy, savagely.

Spike looked at him, amazed.

"Sure," he said, puzzled, but realizing that his words had not pleased the great man.

Jimmy chewed the stem of his pipe irritably, while Spike, full of excellent intentions, sat on the edge of his chair, drawing sorrowfully at his cigar and wondering what he had done to give offense.

"Boss?" said Spike.

"Well?"

"Boss, what's doin' here? Put me next to de game. Is it de old lay? Banks an' jools from duchesses? You'll be able to let me sit in at de game, won't you?"

Jimmy laughed.

"I'd quite forgotten I hadn't told you about myself, Spike. I've retired."

The horrid truth sank slowly into the other's mind.

"Say! What's dat, boss? You're cuttin' it out?"

"That's it. Absolutely."

"Ain't youse swiping no more jools?"

"Not me."

"Nor usin' de what's-its-name blow-pipe?"

"I have sold my oxy-acetylene blow-pipe, given away my anaesthetics, and am going to turn over a new leaf, and settle down as a respectable citizen."

Spike gasped. His world had fallen about his ears. His excursion with. Jimmy, the master cracksman, in New York had been the highest and proudest memory of his life; and, now that they had met again in London, he had looked forward to a long and prosperous partnership in crime. He was content that his own share in the partnership should be humble. It was enough for him to be connected, however humbly, with such a master. He had looked upon the richness of

London, and he had said with Blucher, "What a city to loot!"

And here was his idol shattering the visions with a word.

"Have another drink, Spike," said the lost leader sympathetically. "It's a shock to you, I guess."

"I t'ought, boss - "

"I know, I know. These are life's tragedies. I'm very sorry for you. But it can't be helped. I've made my pile, so why continue?"

Spike sat silent, with a long face. Jimmy slapped him on the shoulder.

"Cheer up," he said. "How do you know that living honestly may not be splendid fun? Numbers of people do it, you know, and enjoy themselves tremendously. You must give it a trial, Spike."

"Me, boss! What, me, too?"

"Sure. You're my link with - I don't want to have you remembering that address in the second month of a ten-year stretch at Dartmoor Prison. I'm going to look after you, Spike, my son, like a lynx. We'll go out together, and see life. Brace up, Spike. Be cheerful. Grin!"

After a moment's reflection, the other grinned, albeit faintly.

"That's right," said Jimmy. "We'll go into society,

Spike, hand in hand. You'll be a terrific success in society. All you have to do is to look cheerful, brush your hair, and keep your hands off the spoons. For in the best circles they invariably count them after the departure of the last guest."

"Sure," said Spike, as one who thoroughly understood this sensible precaution.

"And, now," said Jimmy, "we'll be turning in. Can you manage sleeping on the sofa one night? Some fellows would give their bed up to you. Not me, however. I'll have a bed made up for you tomorrow."

"Me!" said Spike. "Gee! I've been sleepin' in de Park all de last week. Dis is to de good, boss."

CHAPTER XI

AT THE TURN OF THE ROAD

Next morning, when Jimmy, having sent Spike off to the tailor's, with instructions to get a haircut en route, was dealing with a combination of breakfast and luncheon at his flat, Lord Dreever called.

"Thought I should find you in," observed his lordship. "Well, laddie, how goes it? Having breakfast? Eggs and bacon! Great Scott! I couldn't touch a thing."

The statement was borne out by his looks. The son of a hundred earls was pale, and his eyes were markedly fish-like.

"A fellow I've got stopping with me - taking him down to Dreever with me to-day - man I met at the club - fellow named Hargate. Don't know if you know him? No? Well, he was still up when I got back last night, and we stayed up playing billiards - he's rotten at billiards; something frightful: I give him twenty - till five this morning. I feel fearfully cheap. Wouldn't have got up at all, only I'm due to catch the two-fifteen down to Dreever. It's the only good train." He dropped into a chair.

"Sorry you don't feel up to breakfast," said Jimmy,

helping himself to marmalade. "I am generally to be found among those lining up when the gong goes. I've breakfasted on a glass of water and a bag of bird-seed in my time. That sort of thing makes you ready to take whatever you can get. Seen the paper?"

"Thanks."

Jimmy finished his breakfast, and lighted a pipe. Lord Dreever laid down the paper.

"I say," he said, "what I came round about was this. What have you got on just now?"

Jimmy had imagined that his friend had dropped in to return the five-pound note he had borrowed, but his lordship maintained a complete reserve on the subject. Jimmy was to discover later that this weakness of memory where financial obligations were concerned was a leading trait in Lord Dreever's character.

"To-day, do you mean?" said Jimmy.

"Well, in the near future. What I mean is, why not put off that Japan trip you spoke about, and come down to Dreever with me?"

Jimmy reflected. After all, Japan or Dreever, it made very little difference. And it would be interesting to see a place about which he had read so much.

"That's very good of you," he said. "You're sure it will be all right? It won't be upsetting your arrangements?"

"Not a bit. The more the merrier. Can you catch the two-fifteen? It's fearfully short notice."

"Heavens, yes. I can pack in ten minutes. Thanks very much."

"Good business. There'll be shooting and all that sort of rot. Oh, and by the way, are you any good at acting? I mean, there are going to be private theatricals of sorts. A man called Charteris insisted on getting them up - always getting up theatricals. Rot, I call it; but you can't stop him. Do you do anything in that line?"

"Put me down for what you like, from Emperor of Morocco to Confused Noise Without. I was on the stage once. I'm particularly good at shifting scenery."

"Good for you. Well, so long. Two-fifteen from Paddington, remember. I'll meet you there. I've got to go and see a fellow now."

"I'll look out for you."

A sudden thought occurred to Jimmy. Spike! He had forgotten Spike for the moment. It was vital that the Bowery boy should not be lost sight of again. He was the one link with the little house somewhere beyond One Hundred and Fiftieth Street. He could not leave the Bowery boy at the flat. A vision rose in his mind of Spike alone in London, with Savoy Mansions as a base for his operations. No, Spike must be transplanted to the country. But Jimmy could not seem to see Spike in the country. His boredom would probably be pathetic. But it was the only way.

Lord Dreever facilitated matters.

"By the way, Pitt," he said, "you've got a man of sorts, of course? One of those frightful fellows who forgot to pack your collars? Bring him along, of course."

"Thanks," said Jimmy. "I will."

The matter had scarcely been settled when the door opened, and revealed the subject of discussion. Wearing a broad grin of mingled pride and bashfulness, and looking very stiff and awkward in one of the brightest tweed suits ever seen off the stage, Spike stood for a moment in the doorway to let his appearance sink into the spectator, then advanced into the room.

"How do dese strike you, boss?" he inquired genially, as Lord Dreever gaped in astonishment at this bright being.

"Pretty nearly blind, Spike," said Jimmy. "What made you get those? We use electric light here."

Spike was full of news.

"Say, boss, dat clothin'-store's a willy wonder, sure. De old mug what showed me round give me de frozen face when I come in foist. 'What's doin'?' he says. 'To de woods wit' you. Git de hook!' But I hauls out de plunks you give me, an' tells him how I'm here to get a dude suit, an', gee! if he don't haul out suits by de mile. Give me a toist, it did, watching him. 'It's up to youse,' says de mug. 'Choose somet'in'. You pays de money, an' we does de rest.' So, I says dis is de one, an' I put down de plunks, an' here I am, boss."

"I noticed that, Spike," said Jimmy. "I could see you in the dark."

"Don't you like de duds, boss?" inquired Spike, anxiously.

"They're great," said Jimmy. "You'd make Solomon in all his glory look like a tramp 'cyclist."

"Dat's right," agreed Spike. "Dey'se de limit."

And, apparently oblivious to the presence of Lord Dreever, who had been watching him in blank silence since his entrance, the Bowery boy proceeded to execute a mysterious shuffling dance on the carpet.

This was too much for the overwrought brain of his lordship.

"Good-bye, Pitt," he said, "I'm off. Got to see a man."

Jimmy saw his guest to the door.

Outside, Lord Dreever placed the palm of his right hand on his forehead.

"I say, Pitt," he said.

"Hullo?"

"Who the devil's that?"

"Who? Spike? Oh, that's my man."

"Your man! Is he always like that? I mean, going on like a frightful music-hall comedian? Dancing, you know! And, I say, what on earth language was that he was talking? I couldn't understand one word in ten."

"Oh, that's American, the Bowery variety."

"Oh, well, I suppose it's all right if you understand it. I can't. By gad," he broke off, with a chuckle, "I'd give something to see him talking to old Saunders, our butler at home. He's got the manners of a duke."

"Spike should revise those," said Jimmy.

"What do you call him?"

"Spike."

"Rummy name, isn't it?"

"Oh, I don't know. Short for Algernon."

"He seemed pretty chummy."

"That's his independent bringing-up. We're all like that in America."

"Well, so long."

"So long."

On the bottom step, Lord Dreever halted.

"I say. I've got it!"

"Good for you. Got what?"

"Why, I knew I'd seen that chap's face somewhere before, only I couldn't place him. I've got him now. He's the Johnny who came into the shelter last night. Chap you gave a quid to."

P.G. Wodehouse

Spike's was one of those faces that, without being essentially beautiful, stamp themselves on the memory.

"You're quite right," said Jimmy. "I was wondering if you would recognize him. The fact is, he's a man I once employed over in New York, and, when I came across him over here, he was so evidently wanting a bit of help that I took him on again. As a matter of fact, I needed somebody to look after my things, and Spike can do it as well as anybody else."

"I see. Not bad my spotting him, was it? Well, I must be off. Good-bye. Two-fifteen at Paddington. Meet you there. Take a ticket for Dreever if you're there before me."

"Eight. Good-bye."

Jimmy returned to the dining-room. Spike, who was examining as much as he could of himself in the glass, turned round with his wonted grin.

"Say, who's de gazebo, boss? Ain't he de mug youse was wit' last night?"

"That's the man. We're going down with him to the country to-day, Spike, so be ready."

"On your way, boss. What's dat?"

"He has invited us to his country house, and we're going."

"What? Bot'of us?"

"Yes. I told him you were my servant. I hope you aren't offended."

"Nit. What's dere to be raw about, boss?"

"That's all right. Well, we'd better be packing. We have to be at the station at two."

"Sure."

"And, Spike!"

"Yes, boss?"

"Did you get any other clothes besides what you've got on?"

"Nit. What do I want wit more dan one dude suit?"

"I approve of your rugged simplicity," said Jimmy, "but what you're wearing is a town suit. Excellent for the Park or the Marchioness's Thursday crush, but essentially metropolitan. You must get something else for the country, something dark and quiet. I'll come and help you choose it, now."

"Why, won't dis go in de country?"

"Not on your life, Spike. It would unsettle the rustic mind. They're fearfully particular about that sort of thing in England."

"Dey's to de bad," said the baffled disciple of Beau Brummel, with deep discontent.

"And there's just one more thing, Spike. I know you'll

excuse my mentioning it. When we're at Dreever Castle, you will find yourself within reach of a good deal of silver and other things. Would it be too much to ask you to forget your professional instincts? I mentioned this before in a general sort of way, but this is a particular case."

"Ain't I to get busy at all, den?" queried Spike.

"Not so much as a salt-spoon," said Jimmy, firmly. "Now, we'll whistle a cab, and go and choose you some more clothes."

Accompanied by Spike, who came within an ace of looking almost respectable in new blue serge ("Small Gent's" - off the peg), Jimmy arrived at Paddington Station with a quarter of an hour to spare. Lord Dreever appeared ten minutes later, accompanied by a man of about Jimmy's age. He was tall and thin, with cold eyes and tight, thin lips. His clothes fitted him in the way clothes do fit one man in a thousand. They were the best part of him. His general appearance gave one the idea that his meals did him little good, and his meditations rather less. He had practically no conversation.

This was Lord Dreever's friend, Hargate. Lord Dreever made the introductions; but, even as they shook hands, Jimmy had an impression that he had seen the man before. Yet, where or in what circumstances he could not remember. Hargate appeared to have no recollection of him, so he did not mention the matter. A man who has led a wandering life often sees faces that come back to him later on, absolutely detatched from their context. He might merely have passed Lord Dreever's friend on the street. But Jimmy had an idea that the other had figured in some episode which at the moment had had an importance. What that episode was had escaped him. He dismissed the thing from his mind. It was not worth harrying his memory about.

Judicious tipping secured the three a compartment to themselves. Hargate, having read the evening paper, went to sleep in the far corner. Jimmy and Lord Dreever, who sat opposite each other, fell into a desultory conversation.

After awhile, Lord Dreever's remarks took a somewhat intimate turn. Jimmy was one of those men whose manner invites confidences. His lordship began to unburden his soul of certain facts relating to the family.

"Have you ever met my Uncle Thomas?" he inquired. "You know Blunt's Stores? Well, he's Blunt. It's a company now, but he still runs it. He married my aunt. You'll meet him at Dreever."

Jimmy said he would be delighted.

"I bet you won't," said the last of the Dreevers, with candor. "He's a frightful man - the limit. Always fussing round like a hen. Gives me a fearful time, I can. tell you. Look here, I don't mind telling you - we're pals - he's dead set on my marrying a rich girl."

"Well, that sounds all right. There are worse hobbies. Any particular rich girl?"

"There's always one. He sicks me on to one after another. Quite nice girls, you know, some of them;

only, I want to marry somebody else, that girl you saw me with at the Savoy."

"Why don't you tell your uncle?"

"He'd have a fit. She hasn't a penny; nor have I, except what I get from him. Of course, this is strictly between ourselves."

"Of course."

"I know everybody thinks there's money attached to the title; but there isn't, not a penny. When my Aunt Julia married Sir Thomas, the whole frightful show was pretty well in pawn. So, you see how it is."

"Ever think of work?" asked Jimmy.

"Work?" said Lord Dreever, reflectively. "Well, you know, I shouldn't mind work, only I'm dashed if I can see what I could do. I shouldn't know how. Nowadays, you want a fearful specialized education, and so on. Tell you what, though, I shouldn't mind the diplomatic service. One of these days, I shall have a dash at asking my uncle to put up the money. I believe I shouldn't be half-bad at that. I'm rather a quick sort of chap at times, you know. Lots of fellows have said so."

He cleared his throat modestly, and proceeded.

"It isn't only my Uncle Thomas," he said. "There's Aunt Julia, too. She's about as much the limit as he is. I remember, when I was a kid, she was always sitting on me. She does still. Wait till you see her. Sort of woman who makes you feel that your hands are the color of tomatoes and the size of legs of mutton, if you know what I mean. And talks as if she were biting at you. Frightful!"

Having unburdened himself of these criticisms, Lord Dreever yawned, leaned back, and was presently asleep.

It was about an hour later that the train, which had been taking itself less seriously for some time, stopping at stations of quite minor importance and generally showing a tendency to dawdle, halted again. A board with the legend, "Dreever," in large letters showed that they had reached their destination.

The station-master informed Lord Dreever that her ladyship had come to meet the train in the motorcar, and was now waiting in the road outside.

Lord Dreever's jaw fell.

"Oh, lord!" he said. "She's probably motored in to get the afternoon letters. That means, she's come in the runabout, and there's only room for two of us in that. I forgot to telegraph that you were coming, Pitt. I only wired about Hargate. Dash it, I shall have to walk."

His fears proved correct. The car at the station door was small. It was obviously designed to seat four only.

Lord Dreever introduced Hargate and Jimmy to the statuesque lady in the tonneau; and then there was an awkward silence.

At this point, Spike came up, chuckling amiably, with a magazine in his hand.

"Gee!" said Spike. "Say, boss, de mug what wrote dis piece must have bin livin' out in de woods. Say, dere's a gazebo what wants to swipe de heroine's jools what's locked in a drawer. So, dis mug, what 'do you t'ink he does?" Spike laughed shortly, in professional scorn. "Why - "

"Is this gentleman a friend of yours, Spennie?" inquired Lady Julia politely, eying the red-haired speaker coldly.

"It's - " Spennie looked appealingly at Jimmy.

"It's my man," said Jimmy. "Spike," he added in an undertone, "to the woods. Chase yourself. Fade away."

"Sure," said the abashed Spike. "Dat's right. It ain't up to me to come buttin' in. Sorry, boss. Sorry, gents. Sorry loidy. Me for de tall grass."

"There's a luggage-cart of sorts," said Lord Dreever, pointing.

"Sure," said Spike, affably. He trotted away.

"Jump in, Pitt," said Lord Dreever. "I'm going to walk."

"No, I'll walk," said Jimmy. "I'd rather. I want a bit of exercise. Which way do I go?"

"Frightfully good of you, old chap," said Lord Dreever. "Sure you don't mind? I do bar walking. Right-ho! You keep straight on."

He sat down in the tonneau by his aunt's side. The last

Jimmy saw was a hasty vision of him engaged in earnest conversation with Lady Julia. He did not seem to be enjoying himself. Nobody is at his best in conversation with a lady whom he knows to be possessed of a firm belief in the weakness of his intellect. A prolonged conversation with Lady Julia always made Lord Dreever feel as if he were being tied into knots.

Jimmy watched them out of sight, and started to follow at a leisurely pace. It certainly was an ideal afternoon for a country walk. The sun was just hesitating whether to treat the time as afternoon or evening. Eventually, it decided that it was evening, and moderated its beams. After London, the country was deliciously fresh and cool. Jimmy felt an unwonted content. It seemed to him just then that the only thing worth doing in the world was to settle down somewhere with three acres and a cow, and become pastoral.

There was a marked lack of traffic on the road. Once he met a cart, and once a flock of sheep with a friendly dog. Sometimes, a rabbit would dash out into the road, stop to listen, and dart into the opposite hedge, all hind-legs and white scut. But, except for these, he was alone in the world.

And, gradually, there began to be borne in upon him the conviction that he had lost his way.

It is difficult to judge distance when one is walking, but it certainly seemed to Jimmy that he must have covered five miles by this time. He must have mistaken the way. He had doubtless come straight. He could not have come straighter. On the other hand, it would be quite in keeping with the cheap substitute which served the Earl of Dreever in place of a mind that he should have forgotten to mention some important turning. Jimmy sat down by the roadside.

As he sat, there came to him from down the road the sound of a horse's feet, trotting. He got up. Here was somebody at last who would direct him.

The sound came nearer. The horse turned the corner; and Jimmy saw with surprise that it bore no rider.

"Hullo?" he said. "Accident? And, by Jove, a side-saddle!"

The curious part of it was that the horse appeared in no way a wild horse. It gave the impression of being out for a little trot on its own account, a sort of equine constitutional.

Jimmy stopped the horse, and led it back the way it had come. As he turned the bend in the road, he saw a girl in a riding-habit running toward him. She stopped running when she caught sight of him, and slowed down to a walk.

"Thank you ever so much," she said, taking the reins from him. "Dandy, you naughty old thing! I got off to pick up my crop, and he ran away."

Jimmy looked at her flushed, smiling face, and stood staring.

It was Molly McEachern.

CHAPTER XII

MAKING A START

Self-possession was one of Jimmy's leading characteristics, but for the moment he found himself speechless. This girl had been occupying his thoughts for so long that - in his mind - he had grown very intimate with her. It was something of a shock to come suddenly out of his dreams, and face the fact that she was in reality practically a stranger. He felt as one might with a friend whose memory has been wiped out. It went against the grain to have to begin again from the beginning after all the time they had been together.

A curious constraint fell upon him.

"Why, how do you do, Mr. Pitt?" she said, holding out her hand.

Jimmy began to feel better. It was something that she remembered his name.

"It's like meeting somebody out of a dream," said Molly. "I have sometimes wondered if you were real. Everything that happened that night was so like a dream."

P.G. Wodehouse

Jimmy found his tongue.

"You haven't altered," he said, "you look just the same."

"Well," she laughed, "after all, it's not so long ago, is it?"

He was conscious of a dull hurt. To him, it had seemed years. But he was nothing to her - just an acquaintance, one of a hundred. But what more, he asked himself, could he have expected? And with the thought came consolation. The painful sense of having lost ground left him. He saw that he had been allowing things to get out of proportion. He had not lost ground. He had gained it. He had met her again, and she remembered him. What more had he any right to ask?

"I've crammed a good deal into the time," he explained. "I've been traveling about a bit since we met."

"Do you live in Shropshire?" asked Molly.

"No. I'm on a visit. At least, I'm supposed to be. But I've lost the way to the place, and I am beginning to doubt if I shall ever get there. I was told to go straight on. I've gone straight on, and here I am, lost in the snow. Do you happen to know whereabouts Dreever Castle is?"

She laughed.

"Why," she said, "I am staying at Dreever Castle, myself."

"What?"

"So, the first person you meet turns out to be an experienced guide. You're lucky, Mr. Pitt."

"You're right," said Jimmy slowly, "I am."

"Did you come down with Lord Dreever? He passed me in the car just as I was starting out. He was with another man and Lady Julia Blunt. Surely, he didn't make you walk?"

"I offered to walk. Somebody had to. Apparently, he had forgotten to let them know he was bringing me."

"And then he misdirected you! He's very casual, I'm afraid."

"Inclined that way, perhaps."

"Have you known Lord Dreever long?"

"Since a quarter past twelve last night."

"Last night!"

"We met at the Savoy, and, later, on the Embankment. We looked at the river together, and told each other the painful stories of our lives, and this morning he called, and invited me down here."

Molly looked at him with frank amusement.

"You must be a very restless sort of person," she said. "You seem to do a great deal of moving about."

"I do," said Jimmy. "I can't keep still. I've got the go-fever, like that man in Kipling's book."

"But he was in love."

"Yes," said Jimmy. "He was. That's the bacillus, you know."

She shot a quick glance at him. He became suddenly interesting to her. She was at the age of dreams and speculations. From being merely an ordinary young man with rather more ease of manner than the majority of the young men she had met, he developed in an instant into something worthy of closer attention. He took on a certain mystery and romance. She wondered what sort of girl it was that he loved. Examining him in the light of this new discovery, she found him attractive. Something seemed to have happened to put her in sympathy with him. She noticed for the first time a latent forcefulness behind the pleasantness of his manner. His self-possession was the self-possession of the man who has been tried and has found himself.

At the bottom of her consciousness, too, there was a faint stirring of some emotion, which she could not analyze, not unlike pain. It was vaguely reminiscent of the agony of loneliness which she had experienced as a small child on the rare occasions when her father had been busy and distrait, and had shown her by his manner that she was outside his thoughts. This was but a pale suggestion of that misery; nevertheless, there was a resemblance. It was a rather desolate, shut-out sensation, half-resentful.

It was gone in a moment. But it had been there. It had passed over her heart as the shadow of a cloud moves across a meadow in the summer-time.

For some moments, she stood without speaking. Jimmy did not break the silence. He was looking at her with an appeal in his eyes. Why could she not understand? She must understand.

But the eyes that met his were those of a child.

As they stood there, the horse, which had been cropping in a perfunctory manner at the short grass by the roadside, raised its head, and neighed impatiently. There was something so human about the performance that Jimmy and the girl laughed simultaneously. The utter materialism of the neigh broke the spell. It was a noisy demand for food.

"Poor Dandy!" said Molly. "He knows he's near home, and he knows it's his dinner-time."

"Are we near the castle, then?"

"It's a long way round by the road, but we can cut across the fields. Aren't these English fields and hedges just perfect! I love them. Of course, I loved America, but - "

"Have you left New York long?" asked Jimmy.

"We came over here about a month after you were at our house."

"You didn't spend much time there, then."

"Father had just made a good deal of money in Wall Street. He must have been making it when I was on the

Lusitania. He wanted to leave New York, so we didn't wait. We were in London all the winter. Then, we went over to Paris. It was there we met Sir Thomas Blunt and Lady Julia. Have you met them? They are Lord Dreever's uncle and aunt."

"I've met Lady Julia."

"Do you like her?"

Jimmy hesitated.

"Well, you see - "

"I know. She's your hostess, but you haven't started your visit yet. So, you've just got time to say what you really think of her, before you have to pretend she's perfect."

"Well - "

"I detest her," said Molly, crisply. "I think she's hard and hateful."

"Well, I can't say she struck me as a sort of female Cheeryble Brother. Lord Dreever introduced me to her at the station. She seemed to bear it pluckily, but with some difficulty."

"She's hateful," repeated Molly. "So is he, Sir Thomas, I mean. He's one of those fussy, bullying little men. They both bully poor Lord Dreever till I wonder he doesn't rebel. They treat him like a school-boy. It makes me wild. It's such a shame - he's so nice and good-natured! I am so sorry for him!"

Jimmy listened to this outburst with mixed feelings. It was sweet of her to be so sympathetic, but was it merely sympathy? There had been a ring in her voice and a flush on her cheek that had suggested to Jimmy's sensitive mind a personal interest in the down-trodden peer. Reason told him that it was foolish to be jealous of Lord Dreever, a good fellow, of course, but not to be taken seriously. The primitive man in him, on the other hand, made him hate all Molly's male friends with an unreasoning hatred. Not that he hated Lord Dreever: he liked him. But he doubted if he could go on liking him for long if Molly were to continue in this sympathetic strain.

His affection for the absent one was not put to the test. Molly's next remark had to do with Sir Thomas.

"The worst of it is," she said, "father and Sir Thomas are such friends. In Paris, they were always together. Father did him a very good turn."

"How was that?"

"It was one afternoon, just after we arrived. A man got into Lady Julia's room while we were all out except father. Father saw him go into the room, and suspected something was wrong, and went in after him. The man was trying to steal Lady Julia's jewels. He had opened the box where they were kept, and was actually holding her rope of diamonds in his hand when father found him. It's the most magnificent thing I ever saw. Sir Thomas told father he gave a hundred thousand dollars for it."

"But, surely," said Jimmy, "hadn't the management of the hotel a safe for valuables?"

"Of course, they had; but you don't know Sir Thomas. He wasn't going to trust any hotel safe. He's the sort of a man who insists on doing everything in his own way, and who always imagines he can do things better himself than anyone else can do them for him. He had had this special box made, and would never keep the diamonds anywhere else. Naturally, the thief opened it in a minute. A clever thief would have no difficulty with a thing like that."

"What happened?"

"Oh, the man saw father, and dropped the jewels, and ran off down the corridor. Father chased him a little way, but of course it was no good; so he went back and shouted, and rang every bell he could see, and gave the alarm; but the man was never found. Still, he left the diamonds. That was the great thing, after all. You must look at them to-night at dinner. They really are wonderful. Are you a judge of precious stones at all?"

"I am rather," said Jimmy. "In fact, a jeweler I once knew told me I had a natural gift in that direction. And so, of course, Sir Thomas was pretty grateful to your father?"

"He simply gushed. He couldn't do enough for him. You see, if the diamonds had been stolen, I'm sure Lady Julia would have made Sir Thomas buy her another rope just as good. He's terrified of her, I'm certain. He tries not to show it, but he is. And, besides having to pay another hundred thousand dollars, he would never have heard the last of it. It would have ruined his reputation for being infallible and doing everything better than anybody else."

"But didn't the mere fact that the thief got the jewels, and was only stopped by a fluke from getting away with them, do that?"

Molly bubbled with laughter.

"She never knew. Sir Thomas got back to the hotel an hour before she did. I've never seen such a busy hour. He had the manager up, harangued him, and swore him to secrecy - which the poor manager was only too glad to agree to, because it wouldn't have done the hotel any good to have it known. And the manager harangued the servants, and the servants harangued one another, and everybody talked at the same time; and father and I promised not to tell a soul; so Lady Julia doesn't know a word about it to this day. And I don't see why she ever should - though, one of these days, I've a good mind to tell Lord Dreever. Think what a hold he would have over them! They'd never be able to bully him again."

"I shouldn't," said Jimmy, trying to keep a touch of coldness out of his voice. This championship of Lord Dreever, however sweet and admirable, was a little distressing.

She looked up quickly.

"You don't think I really meant to, do you?"

"No, no," said Jimmy, hastily. "Of course not."

"Well, I should think so!" said Molly, indignantly. "After I promised not to tell a soul about it!"

Jimmy chuckled.

"It's nothing," he said, in answer to her look of inquiry.

"You laughed at something."

"Well," said Jimmy apologetically, "it's only - it's nothing really - only, what I mean is, you have just told one soul a good deal about it, haven't you?"

Molly turned pink. Then, she smiled.

"I don't know how I came to do it," she declared. "It just rushed out of its own accord. I suppose it is because I know I can trust you."

Jimmy flushed with pleasure. He turned to her, and half-halted, but she continued to walk on.

"You can," he said, "but how do you know you can?"

She seemed surprised.

"Why - " she said. She stopped for a moment, and then went on hurriedly, with a touch of embarrassment. "Why, how absurd! Of course, I know. Can't you read faces? I can. Look," she said, pointing, "now you can see the castle. How do you like it?"

They had reached a point where the fields sloped sharply downward. A few hundred yards away, backed by woods, stood the gray mass of stone which had proved such a kill-joy of old to the Welsh sportsmen during the pheasant season. Even now, it had a certain air of defiance. The setting sun lighted the waters of the lake. No figures were to be seen moving in the grounds. The place resembled a palace of sleep.

"Well?" said Molly.

"It's wonderful!"

"Isn't it! I'm so glad it strikes you like that. I always feel as if I had invented everything round here. It hurts me if people don't appreciate it."

They went down the hill.

"By the way," said Jimmy, "are you acting in these theatricals they are getting up?"

"Yes. Are you the other man they were going to get? That's why Lord Dreever went up to London, to see if he couldn't find somebody. The man who was going to play one of the parts had to go back to London on business."

"Poor brute!" said Jimmy. It seemed to him at this moment that there was only one place in the world where a man might be even reasonably happy. "What sort of part is it? Lord Dreever said I should be wanted to act. What do I do?"

"If you're Lord Herbert, which is the part they wanted a man for, you talk to me most of the time."

Jimmy decided that the piece had been well cast.

The dressing-gong sounded just as they entered the hall. From a door on the left, there emerged two men, a big man and a little one, in friendly conversation. The big man's back struck Jimmy as familiar.

"Oh, father," Molly called. And Jimmy knew where he

had seen the back before.

The two men stopped.

"Sir Thomas," said Molly, "this is Mr. Pitt."

The little man gave Jimmy a rapid glance, possibly with the object of detecting his more immediately obvious criminal points; then, as if satisfied as to his honesty, became genial.

"I am very glad to meet you, Mr. Pitt, very glad," he said. "We have been expecting you for some time."

Jimmy explained that he had lost his way.

"Exactly. It was ridiculous that you should be compelled to walk, perfectly ridiculous. It was grossly careless of my nephew not to let us know that you were coming. My wife told him so in the car."

"I bet she did," said Jimmy to himself. "Really," he said aloud, by way of lending a helping hand to a friend in trouble, "I preferred to walk. I have not been on a country road since I landed in England." He turned to the big man, and held out his hand. "I don't suppose you remember me, Mr. McEachern? We met in New York."

"You remember the night Mr. Pitt scared away our burglar, father," said Molly.

Mr. McEachern was momentarily silent. On his native asphalt, there are few situations capable of throwing the New York policeman off his balance. In that favored clime, savoir faire is represented by a shrewd blow of the fist, and a masterful stroke with the truncheon amounts to a satisfactory repartee. Thus shall you never take the policeman of Manhattan without his answer. In other surroundings, Mr. McEachern would have known how to deal with the young man whom with such good reason he believed to be an expert criminal. But another plan of action was needed here. First and foremost, of all the hints on etiquette that he had imbibed since he entered this more reposeful life, came the maxim: "Never make a scene." Scenes, he had gathered, were of all things what polite society most resolutely abhorred. The natural man in him must be bound in chains. The sturdy blow must give way to the honeyed word. A cold, "Really!" was the most vigorous retort that the best circles would countenance. It had cost Mr. McEachern some pains to learn this lesson, but he had done it. He shook hands, and gruffly acknowledged the acquaintanceship.

"Really, really!" chirped Sir Thomas, amiably. "So, you find yourself among old friends, Mr. Pitt."

"Old friends," echoed Jimmy, painfully conscious of the ex-policeman's eyes, which were boring holes in him.

"Excellent, excellent! Let me take you to your room. It is just opposite my own. This way."

In his younger days, Sir Thomas had been a floor-walker of no mean caliber. A touch of the professional still lingered in his brisk movements. He preceded Jimmy upstairs with the restrained suavity that can be learned in no other school.

They parted from Mr. McEachern on the first landing,

but Jimmy could still feel those eyes. The policeman's stare had been of the sort that turns corners, goes upstairs, and pierces walls.

CHAPTER XIII

SPIKE'S VIEWS

Nevertheless, it was in an exalted frame of mind that Jimmy dressed for dinner. It seemed to him that he had awakened from a sort of stupor. Life, so gray yesterday, now appeared full of color and possibilities. Most men who either from choice or necessity have knocked about the world for any length of time are more or less fatalists. Jimmy was an optimistic fatalist. He had always looked on Fate, not as a blind dispenser at random of gifts good and bad, but rather as a benevolent being with a pleasing bias in his own favor. He had almost a Napoleonic faith in his star. At various periods of his life (notably at the time when, as he had told Lord Dreever, he had breakfasted on birdseed), he had been in uncommonly tight corners, but his luck had always extricated him. It struck him that it would be an unthinkable piece of bad sportsmanship on Fate's part to see him through so much, and then to abandon him just as he had arrived in sight of what was by far the biggest thing of his life. Of course, his view of what constituted the biggest thing in life had changed with the years. Every ridge of the Hill of Supreme Moments in turn had been mistaken by him for the summit; but this last, he felt instinctively, was genuine. For good or bad, Molly was woven into the texture of his life. In the stormy period of the early

P.G. Wodehouse

twenties, he had thought the same of other girls, who were now mere memories as dim as those of figures in a half-forgotten play. In their case, his convalescence had been temporarily painful, but brief. Force of will and an active life had worked the cure. He had merely braced himself, and firmly ejected them from his mind. A week or two of aching emptiness, and his heart had been once more in readiness, all nicely swept and garnished, for the next lodger.

But, in the case of Molly, it was different. He had passed the age of instantaneous susceptibility. Like a landlord who has been cheated by previous tenants, he had become wary. He mistrusted his powers of recuperation in case of disaster. The will in these matters, just like the mundane "bouncer," gets past its work. For some years now, Jimmy had had a feeling that the next arrival would come to stay; and he had adopted in consequence a gently defensive attitude toward the other sex. Molly had broken through this, and he saw that his estimate of his will-power had been just. Methods that had proved excellent in the past were useless now. There was no trace here of the dimly consoling feeling of earlier years, that there were other girls in the world. He did not try to deceive himself. He knew that he had passed the age when a man can fall in love with any one of a number of types.

This was the finish, one way or the other. There would be no second throw. She had him. However it might end, he belonged to her.

There are few moments in a man's day when his brain is more contemplative than during that brief space when he is lathering his face, preparatory to shaving. Plying the brush, Jimmy reviewed the situation. He was, perhaps, a little too optimistic. Not unnaturally, he was inclined to look upon his luck as a sort of special train which would convey him without effort to Paradise. Fate had behaved so exceedingly handsomely up till now! By a series of the most workmanlike miracles, it had brought him to the point of being Molly's fellow-guest at a country-house. This, as reason coldly pointed out a few moments later, was merely the beginning, but to Jimmy, thoughtfully lathering, it seemed the end. It was only when he had finished shaving, and was tying his cravat, that he began to perceive obstacles in his way, and sufficiently big obstacles, at that.

In the first place, Molly did not love him. And, he was bound to admit, there was no earthly reason why she ever should. A man in love is seldom vain about his personal attractions. Also, her father firmly believed him to be a master-burglar.

"Otherwise," said Jimmy, scowling at his reflection in the glass, "everything's splendid." He brushed his hair sadly.

There was a furtive rap at the door.

"Hullo?" said Jimmy. "Yes?"

The door opened slowly. A grin, surmounted by a mop of red hair, appeared round the edge of it.

"Hullo, Spike. Come in. What's the matter?"

The rest of Mr. Mullins entered the room.

"Gee, boss! I wasn't sure was dis your room. Say, who

P.G. Wodehouse

do you t'ink I nearly bumped me coco ag'inst out in de corridor downstairs? Why, old man McEachern, de cop. Dat's right!"

"Yes?"

"Sure. Say, what's he doin' on dis beat? I pretty near went down an' out when I seen him. Dat's right. Me breath ain't got back home yet."

"Did he recognize you?"

"Did he! He starts like an actor on top de stoige when he sees he's up ag'inst de plot to ruin him, an' he gives me de fierce eye."

"Well?"

"I was wonderin' was I on Thoid Avenoo, or was I standin' on me coco, or what was I doin' anyhow. Den I slips off, an' chases meself up here. Say, boss, what's de game? What's old man McEachern doin' stunts dis side fer?"

"It's all right, Spike. Keep calm. I can explain. He has retired -
like me! He's one of the handsome guests here."

"On your way, boss! What's dat?"

"He left the force just after that merry meeting of ours when you frolicked with the bull-dog. He came over here, and butted into society. So, here we are again, all gathered together under the same roof, like a jolly little family party."

Spike's open mouth bore witness to his amazement.

"Den - " he stammered.

"Yes?"

"Den, what's be goin' to do?"

"I couldn't say. I'm expecting to hear shortly. But we needn't worry ourselves. The next move's with him. If he wants to comment on the situation, he won't be backward. He'll come and do it."

"Sure. It's up to him," agreed Spike.

"I'm quite comfortable. Speaking for myself, I'm having a good time. How are you getting along downstairs?"

"De limit, boss. Honest, it's to de velvet. Dey's an old gazebo, de butler, Saunders his name is, dat's de best ever at handin' out long woids. I sits an' listens. Dey calls me Mr. Mullins down dere," said Spike, with pride.

"Good. I'm glad you're all right. There's no season why we shouldn't have an excellent time here. I don't think that Mr. McEachern will try to have us turned out, after he's heard one or two little things I have to say to him - just a few reminiscences of the past which may interest him. I have the greatest affection for Mr. McEachern - I wish it were mutual - but nothing he can say is going to make me stir from here."

"Not on your life," agreed Spike. "Say, boss, he must have got a lot of plunks to be able to butt in here. An' I know how he got dem, too. Dat's right. I comes from little old New York, meself."

"Hush, Spike, this is scandal!"

"Sure," said the Bowery boy doggedly, safely started now on his favorite subject. "I knows, an' youse knows, boss. Gee! I wish I'd bin a cop. But I wasn't tall enough. Dey's de fellers wit' de big bank-rolls. Look at dis old McEachern. Money to boin a wet dog wit' he's got, an' never a bit of woik fer it from de start to de finish. An' look at me, boss."

"I do, Spike, I do."

"Look at me. Gittin' busy all de year round, woikin' to beat de band - "

"In prisons oft," said Jimmy.

"Sure t'ing. An' chased all roun' de town. An' den what? Why, to de bad at de end of it all. Say, it's enough to make a feller - "

"Turn honest," said Jimmy. "That's it, Spike. Reform. You'll be glad some day."

Spike seemed to be doubtful. He was silent for a moment, then, as if following up a train of thought, he said:

"Boss, dis is a fine big house."

"I've seen worse."

"Say, couldn't we - ?"

"Spike!" said Jimmy, warningly.

"Well, couldn't we?" said Spike, doggedly. "It ain't often youse butts into a dead-easy proposition like dis one. We shouldn't have to do a t'ing excep' git busy. De stuff's just lyin' about, boss."

"I shouldn't wonder."

"Aw, it's a waste to leave it."

"Spike," said Jimmy, "I warned you of this. I begged you to be on your guard, to fight against your professional instincts. Be a man! Crush them. Try and occupy your mind. Collect butterflies."

Spike shuffled in gloomy silence.

"'Member dose jools youse swiped from de duchess?" he said, musingly.

"The dear duchess!" murmured Jimmy. "Ah, me!"

"An' de bank youse busted?"

"Those were happy days, Spike."

"Gee!" said the Bowery boy. And then, after a pause: "Dat was to de good," he said, wistfully.

Jimmy arranged his tie at the mirror.

"Dere's a loidy here," continued Spike, addressing the chest of drawers, "dat's got a necklace of jools what's wort' a hundred t'ousand plunks. Honest, boss. A hundred t'ousand plunks. Saunders told me dat - de old

P.G. Wodehouse

gazebo dat hands out de long woids. I says to him, 'Gee!' an' he says, 'Surest t'ing youse know.' A hundred t'ousand plunks!"

"So I understand," said Jimmy.

"Shall I rubber around, an' find out where is dey kept, boss?"

"Spike," said Jimmy, "ask me no more. All this is in direct contravention of our treaty respecting keeping your fingers off the spoons. You pain me. Desist."

"Sorry, boss. But dey'll be willy-wonders, dem jools. A hundred t'ousand plunks. Dat's goin' some, ain't it? What's dat dis side?"

"Twenty thousand pounds."

"Gee!...Can I help youse wit' de duds, boss?"

"No, thanks, Spike, I'm through now. You might just give me a brush down, though. No, not that. That's a hair-brush. Try the big black one."

"Dis is a boid of a dude suit," observed Spike, pausing in his labors.

"Glad you like it, Spike. Rather chic, I think."

"It's de limit. Excuse me. How much did it set youse back, boss?"

"Something like seven guineas, I believe. I could look up the bill, and let you know."

"What's dat - guineas? Is dat more dan a pound?"

"A shilling more. Why these higher mathematics?"

Spike resumed his brushing.

"What a lot of dude suits youse could git," he observed meditatively, "if youse had dem jools!" He became suddenly animated. He waved the clothes-brush. "Oh, you boss!" he cried. "What's eatin' youse? Aw, it's a shame not to. Come along, you boss! Say, what's doin'? Why ain't youse sittin' in at de game? Oh, you boss!"

Whatever reply Jimmy might have made to this impassioned appeal was checked by a sudden bang on the door. Almost simultaneously, the handle turned.

"Gee!" cried Spike. "It's de cop!"

Jimmy smiled pleasantly.

"Come in, Mr. McEachern," he said, "come in. Journeys end in lovers meeting. You know my friend Mr. Mullins, I think? Shut the door, and sit down, and let's talk of many things."

CHAPTER XIV

CHECK AND A COUNTER MOVE

Mr. McEachern stood in the doorway, breathing heavily. As the result of a long connection with evil-doers, the ex-policeman was somewhat prone to harbor suspicions of those round about him, and at the present moment his mind was aflame. Indeed, a more trusting man might have been excused for feeling a little doubtful as to the intentions of Jimmy and Spike. When McEachern had heard that Lord Dreever had brought home a casual London acquaintance, he had suspected as a possible drawback to the visit the existence of hidden motives on the part of the unknown. Lord Dreever, he had felt, was precisely the sort of youth to whom the professional bunco-steerer would attach himself with shouts of joy. Never, he had assured himself, had there been a softer proposition than his lordship since bunco-steering became a profession. When he found that the strange visitor was Jimmy Pitt, his suspicions had increased a thousand-fold.

And when, going to his room to get ready for dinner, he had nearly run into Spike Mullins in the corridor, his frame of mind had been that of a man to whom a sudden ray of light reveals the fact that he is on the brink of a black precipice. Jimmy and Spike had burgled his house together in New York. And here they were, together again, at Dreever Castle. To say that the thing struck McEachern as sinister is to put the matter baldly. There was once a gentleman who remarked that he smelt a rat, and saw it floating in the air. Ex-Constable McEachern smelt a regiment of rats, and the air seemed to him positively congested with them.

His first impulse had been to rush to Jimmy's room there and then; but he had learned society's lessons well. Though the heavens might fall, he must not be late for dinner. So, he went and dressed, and an obstinate tie put the finishing touches to his wrath.

Jimmy regarded him coolly, without moving from, the chair in which he had seated himself. Spike, on the other hand, seemed embarrassed. He stood first on one leg, and then on the other, as if he were testing the respective merits of each, and would make a definite choice later on.

"You scoundrels!" growled McEachern.

Spike, who had been standing for a few moments on his right leg, and seemed at last to have come to, a decision, hastily changed to the left, and grinned feebly.

"Say, youse won't want me any more, boss?" he whispered.

"No, you can go, Spike."

"You stay where you are, you red-headed devil!" said McEachern, tartly.

"Run along, Spike," said Jimmy.

The Bowery boy looked doubtfully at the huge form of the ex-policeman, which blocked access to the door.

"Would you mind letting my man pass?" said Jimmy.

"You stay - " began McEachern.

Jimmy got up and walked round to the door, which he opened. Spike shot out. He was not lacking in courage, but he disliked embarrassing interviews, and it struck him that Jimmy was the man to handle a situation of this kind. He felt that he himself would only be in the way.

"Now, we can talk comfortably," said Jimmy, going back to his chair.

McEachern's deep-set eyes gleamed, and his forehead grew red, but he mastered his feelings.

"And now - " said he, then paused.

"Yes?" asked Jimmy.

"What are you doing here?"

"Nothing, at the moment."

"You know what I mean. Why are you here, you and that red-headed devil, Spike Mullins?" He jerked his head in the direction of the door.

"I am here because I was very kindly invited to come by Lord Dreever."

"I know you."

"You have that privilege. Seeing that we only met once, it's very good of you to remember me."

"What's your game? What do you mean to do?"

"To do? Well, I shall potter about the garden, you know, and shoot a bit, perhaps, and look at the horses, and think of life, and feed the chickens - I suppose there are chickens somewhere about - and possibly go for an occasional row on the lake. Nothing more. Oh, yes, I believe they want me to act in some theatricals."

"You'll miss those theatricals. You'll leave here to-morrow."

"To-morrow? But I've only just arrived, dear heart."

"I don't care about that. Out you go to-morrow. I'll give you till to-morrow."

"I congratulate you," said Jimmy. "One of the oldest houses in England."

"What do you mean?"

"I gathered from what you said that you had bought the Castle. Isn't that so? If it still belongs to Lord Dreever, don't you think you ought to consult him before revising his list of guests?"

McEachern looked steadily at him. His manner became quieter.

"Oh, you take that tone, do you?"

"I don't know what you mean by 'that tone.' What tone would you take if a comparative stranger ordered you to leave another man's house?"

McEachern's massive jaw protruded truculently in the manner that had scared good behavior into brawling East Siders.

"I know your sort," he said. "I'll call your bluff. And you won't get till to-morrow, either. It'll be now."

"'Why should we wait for the morrow? You are queen of my heart to-night," murmured Jimmy, encouragingly.

"I'll expose you before them all. I'll tell them everything."

Jimmy shook his head.

"Too melodramatic," he said. "'I call on heaven to judge between this man and me!' kind of thing. I shouldn't. What do you propose to tell, anyway?"

"Will you deny that you were a crook in New York?"

"I will. I was nothing of the kind."

"What?"

"If you'll listen, I can explain - "

"Explain!" The other's voice rose again. "You talk about explaining, you scum, when I caught you in my own parlor at three in the morning - you - "

The smile faded from Jimmy's face.

"Half a minute," he said. It might be that the ideal course would be to let the storm expend itself, and then to explain quietly the whole matter of Arthur Mifflin and the bet that had led to his one excursion into burglary; but he doubted it. Things - including his temper - had got beyond the stage of quiet explanations. McEachern would most certainly disbelieve his story. What would happen after that he did not know. A scene, probably: a melodramatic denunciation, at the worst, before the other guests; at the best, before Sir Thomas alone. He saw nothing but chaos beyond that. His story was thin to a degree, unless backed by witnesses, and his witnesses were three thousand miles away. Worse, he had not been alone in the policeman's parlor. A man who is burgling a house for a bet does not usually do it in the company of a professional burglar, well known to the police.

No, quiet explanations must be postponed. They could do no good, and would probably lead to his spending the night and the next few nights at the local police-station. And, even if he were spared that fate, it was certain that he would have to leave the castle – leave the castle and Molly!

He jumped up. The thought had stung him.

"One moment," he said.

McEachern stopped.

"Well?"

"You're going to tell them that?" asked Jimmy.

"I am."

Jimmy walked up to him.

"Are you also going to tell them why you didn't have me arrested that night?" he said.

McEachern started. Jimmy planted himself in front of him, and glared up into his face. It would have been hard to say which of the two was the angrier. The policeman was flushed, and the veins stood out on his forehead. Jimmy was in a white heat of rage. He had turned very pale, and his muscles were quivering. Jimmy in this mood had once cleared a Los Angeles bar-room with the leg of a chair in the space of two and a quarter minutes by the clock.

"Are you?" he demanded. "Are you?"

McEachern's hand, hanging at his side, lifted itself hesitatingly. The fingers brushed against Jimmy's shoulder.

Jimmy's lip twitched.

"Yes," he said, "do it! Do it, and see what happens. By God, if you put a hand on me, I'll finish you. Do you think you can bully me? Do you think I care for your size?"

McEachern dropped his hand. For the first time in his life, he had met a man who, instinct told him, was his match and more. He stepped back a pace.

Jimmy put his hands in his pockets, and turned away. He walked to the mantelpiece, and leaned his back against it.

"You haven't answered my question," he said. "Perhaps, you can't?"

McEachern was wiping his forehead, and breathing quickly.

"If you like," said Jimmy, "we'll go down to the drawing-room now, and you shall tell your story, and I'll tell mine. I wonder which they will think the more interesting. Damn you," he went on, his anger rising once more, "what do you mean by it? You come into my room, and bluster, and talk big about exposing crooks. What do you call yourself, I wonder? Do you realize what you are? Why, poor Spike's an angel compared with you. He did take chances. He wasn't in a position of trust. You - "

He stopped.

"Hadn't you better get out of here, don't you think?" he said, curtly.

Without a word, McEachern walked to the door, and went out.

Jimmy dropped into a chair with a deep breath. He took up his cigarette-case, but before he could light a match the gong sounded from the distance.

He rose, and laughed rather shakily. He felt limp. "As an effort at conciliating papa," he said, "I'm afraid that wasn't much of a success."

It was not often that McEachern was visited by ideas.

He ran rather to muscle than to brain. But he had one that evening during dinner. His interview with Jimmy had left him furious, but baffled. He knew that his hands were tied. Frontal attack was useless. To drive Jimmy from the castle would be out of the question. All that could be done was to watch him while he was there. For he had never been more convinced of anything in his life than that Jimmy had wormed his way into the house-party with felonious intent. The appearance of Lady Julia at dinner, wearing the famous rope of diamonds, supplied an obvious motive. The necklace had an international reputation. Probably, there was not a prominent thief in England or on the Continent who had not marked it down as a possible prey. It had already been tried for, once. It was big game, just the sort of lure that would draw the type of criminal McEachern imagined Jimmy to be.

From his seat at the far end of the table, Jimmy looked at the jewels as they gleamed on their wearer's neck. They were almost too ostentatious for what was, after all, an informal dinner. It was not a rope of diamonds. It was a collar. There was something Oriental and barbaric in the overwhelming display of jewelry. It was a prize for which a thief would risk much.

The conversation, becoming general with the fish, was not of a kind to remove from his mind the impression made by the sight of the gems. It turned on burglary.

Lord Dreever began it.

"Oh, I say," he said, "I forgot to tell you, Aunt Julia, Number Six was burgled the other night."

Number 6a, Eaton Square, was the family's London house.

"Burgled!" cried Sir Thomas.

"Well, broken into," said his lordship, gratified to find that he had got the ear of his entire audience. Even Lady Julia was silent and attentive. "Chap got in through the scullery window about one o'clock in the morning."

"And what did you do?" inquired Sir Thomas.

"Oh, I - er - I was out at the time," said Lord Dreever. "But something frightened the feller," he went on hurriedly, "and he made a bolt for it without taking anything."

"Burglary," said a young man, whom Jimmy subsequenttly discovered to be the drama-loving Charteris, leaning back and taking advantage of a pause, "is the hobby of the sportsman and the life work of the avaricious." He took a little pencil from his waistcoat pocket, and made a rapid note on his cuff.

Everybody seemed to have something to say on. the subject. One young lady gave it as her opinion that she would not like to find a burglar under her bed. Somebody else had heard of a fellow whose father had fired at the butler, under the impression that he was a house-breaker, and had broken a valuable bust of Socrates. Lord Dreever had known a man at college whose brother wrote lyrics for musical comedy, and had done one about a burglar's best friend being his mother.

P.G. Wodehouse

"Life," said Charteris, who had had time for reflection, "is a house which we all burgle. We enter it uninvited, take all that we can lay hands on, and go out again." He scribbled, "Life - house - burgle," on his cuff, and replaced the pencil.

"This man's brother I was telling you about," said Lord Dreever, "says there's only one rhyme in the English language to 'burglar,' and that's 'gurgler - ' unless you count 'pergola'! He says - "

"Personally," said Jimmy, with a glance at McEachern, "I have rather a sympathy for burglars. After all, they are one of the hardest-working classes in existence. They toil while everybody else is asleep. Besides, a burglar is only a practical socialist. People talk a lot about the redistribution of wealth. The burglar goes out and does it. I have found burglars some of the decentest criminals I have ever met."

"I despise burglars!" ejaculated Lady Julia, with a suddenness that stopped Jimmy's eloquence as if a tap had been turned off. "If I found one coming after my jewels, and I had a pistol, I'd shoot him."

Jimmy met McEachern's eye, and smiled kindly at him. The ex-policeman was looking at him with the gaze of a baffled, but malignant basilisk.

"I take very good care no one gets a chance at your diamonds, my dear," said Sir Thomas, without a blush. "I have had a steel box made for me," he added to the company in general, "with a special lock. A very ingenious arrangement. Quite unbreakable, I imagine."

Jimmy, with Molly's story fresh in his mind, could not

check a rapid smile. Mr. McEachern, watching intently, saw it. To him, it was fresh evidence, if any had been wanted, of Jimmy's intentions and of his confidence of success. McEachern's brow darkened. During the rest of the meal, tense thought rendered him even more silent than was his wont at the dinner-table. The difficulty of his position was, he saw, great. Jimmy, to be foiled, must be watched, and how could he watch him?

It was not until the coffee arrived that he found an answer to the question. With his first cigarette came the idea. That night, in his room, before going to bed, he wrote a letter. It was an unusual letter, but, singularly enough, almost identical with one Sir Thomas Blunt had written that very morning.

It was addressed to the Manager of Dodson's Private Inquiry Agency, of Bishopsgate Street, E. C., and ran as follows:

Sir, -

On receipt of this, kindly send down one of your smartest men. Instruct him to stay at the village inn in character of American seeing sights of England, and anxious to inspect Dreever Castle. I will meet him in the village and recognize him as old New York friend, and will then give him further instructions. Yours faithfully,

J. McEACHERN.

P. S. Kindly not send a rube, but a real smart man.

This brief, but pregnant letter cost some pains in its composition. McEachern was not a ready writer. But he completed it at last to his satisfaction. There was a crisp purity in the style that pleased him. He sealed up the envelope, and slipped it into his pocket. He felt more at ease now. Such was the friendship that had sprung up between Sir Thomas Blunt and himself as the result of the jewel episode in Paris that he could count with certainty on the successful working of his scheme. The grateful knight would not be likely to allow any old New York friend of his preserver to languish at the village inn. The sleuth-hound would at once be installed at the castle, where, unsuspected by Jimmy, he could keep an eye on the course of events. Any looking after that Mr. James Pitt might require could safely be left in the hands of this expert.

With considerable fervor, Mr. McEachern congratulated himself on his astuteness. With Jimmy above stairs and Spike below, the sleuth-hound would have his hands full.

CHAPTER XV

MR. MCEACHERN INTERVENES

Life at the castle during the first few days of his visit filled Jimmy with a curious blend of emotions, mainly unpleasant. Fate, in its pro-Jimmy capacity, seemed to be taking a rest. In the first place, the part allotted to him was not that of Lord Herbert, the character who talked to Molly most of the time. The instant Charteris learned from Lord Dreever that Jimmy had at one time actually been on the stage professionally, he decided that Lord Herbert offered too little scope for the new man's talents.

"Absolutely no good to you, my dear chap," he said. "It's just a small dude part. He's simply got to be a silly ass."

Jimmy pleaded that he could be a sillier ass than anybody living; but Charteris was firm.

"No," he said. "You must be Captain Browne. Fine acting part. The biggest in the piece. Full of fat lines. Spennie was to have played it, and we were in for the worst frost in the history of the stage. Now you've come, it's all right. Spennie's the ideal Lord Herbert. He's simply got to be him-self. We've got a success now, my boy. Rehearsal after lunch. Don't be late."

And he was off to beat up the rest of the company.

From that moment, Jimmy's troubles began. Charteris was a young man in whom a passion for the stage was ineradicably implanted. It mattered nothing to him during these days that the sun shone, that it was pleasant on the lake, and that Jimmy would have given five pounds a minute to be allowed to get Molly to himself for half-an-hour every afternoon. All he knew or cared about was that the local nobility and gentry were due to arrive at the castle within a week, and that, as yet, very few of the company even knew their lines. Having hustled Jimmy into the part of CAPTAIN BROWNE, he gave his energy free play. He conducted rehearsals with a vigor that occasionally almost welded the rabble he was coaching into something approaching coherency. He painted scenery, and left it about - wet, and people sat on it. He nailed up horseshoes for luck, and they fell on people. But nothing daunted him. He never rested.

"Mr. Charteris," said Lady Julia, rather frigidly, after one energetic rehearsal, "is indefatigable. He whirled me about!"

It was perhaps his greatest triumph, properly considered, that he had induced Lady Julia to take a part in his piece; but to the born organizer of amateur theatricals no miracle of this kind is impossible, and Charteris was one of the most inveterate organizers in the country. There had been some talk - late at night, in the billiard room - of his being about to write in a comic footman role for Sir Thomas; but it had fallen through, not, it was felt, because Charteris could not have hypnotized his host into undertaking the part, but rather because Sir Thomas was histrionically unfit.

Mainly as a result of the producer's energy, Jimmy found himself one of a crowd, and disliked the sensation. He had not experienced much difficulty in mastering the scenes in which lie appeared; but unfortunately those who appeared with him had. It occurred to Jimmy daily, after he had finished "running through the lines" with a series of agitated amateurs, male and female, that for all practical purposes he might just as well have gone to Japan. In this confused welter of rehearsers, his opportunities of talking with Molly were infinitesimal. And, worse, she did not appear to mind. She was cheerful and apparently quite content to be engulfed in a crowd. Probably, he thought with some melancholy, if she met his eye and noted in it a distracted gleam, she put it down to the cause that made other eyes in the company gleam distractedly during this week.

Jimmy began to take a thoroughly jaundiced view of amateur theatricals, and of these amateur theatricals in particular. He felt that in the electric flame department of the infernal regions there should be a special gridiron, reserved exclusively for the man who invented these performances, so diametrically opposed to the true spirit of civilization. At the close of each day, he cursed Charteris with unfailing regularity.

There was another thing that disturbed him. That he should be unable to talk with Molly was an evil, but a negative evil. It was supplemented by one that was positive. Even in the midst of the chaos of rehearsals, he could not help noticing that Molly and Lord Dreever were very much together. Also - and this was even more sinister - he observed that both Sir Thomas Blunt and Mr. McEachern were making determined efforts to foster the state of affairs.

Of this, he had sufficient proof one evening when, after scheming and plotting in a way that had made the great efforts of Machiavelli and Eichlieu seem like the work of raw novices, he had cut Molly out from the throng, and carried her off for the alleged purpose of helping him feed the chickens. There were, as he had suspected, chickens attached to the castle. They lived in a little world of noise and smells at the back of the stables. Bearing an iron pot full of a poisonous-looking mash, and accompanied by Molly, he had felt for perhaps a minute and a half like a successful general. It is difficult to be romantic when you are laden with chicken-feed in an unwieldy iron pot, but he had resolved that this portion of the proceedings should be brief. The birds should dine that evening on the quick-lunch principle. Then - to the more fitting surroundings of the rose-garden! There was plenty of time before the hour of the sounding of the dressing-gong. Perhaps, even a row on the lake - "What ho!" said a voice.

Behind them, with a propitiatory smile on his face, stood his lordship of Dreever.

"My uncle told me I should find you out here. What have you got in there, Pitt? Is this what you feed them on? I say, you know, queer coves, hens! I wouldn't touch that stuff for a fortune, what? Looks to me poisonous."

He met Jimmy's eye, and stopped. There was that in Jimmy's eye that would have stopped an avalanche. His lordship twiddled his fingers in pink embarrassment.

"Oh, look!" said Molly. "There's a poor little chicken out there in the cold. It hasn't had a morsel. Give me

the spoon, Mr. Pitt. Here, chick, chick! Don't be silly,
I'm not going to hurt you. I've brought you your
dinner."

She moved off in pursuit of the solitary fowl, which
had edged nervously away. Lord Dreever bent toward
Jimmy.

"Frightfully sorry, Pitt, old man," he whispered,
feverishly. "Didn't want to come. Couldn't help it. He
sent me out." He half-looked over his shoulder. "And,"
he added rapidly, as Molly came back, "the old boy's
up at his bedroom window now, watching us through
his opera-glasses!"

The return journey to the house was performed in
silence - on Jimmy's part, in thoughtful silence. He
thought hard, and he had been thinking ever since.

He had material for thought. That Lord Dreever was as
clay in his uncle's hands he was aware. He had not
known his lordship long, but he had known him long
enough to realize that a backbone had been carelessly
omitted from his composition. What his uncle directed,
that would he do. The situation looked bad to Jimmy.
The order, he knew, had gone out that Lord Dreever
was to marry money. And Molly was an heiress. He
did not know how much Mr. McEachern had amassed
in his dealings with New York crime, but it must be
something considerable. Things looked black.

Then, Jimmy had a reaction. He was taking much for
granted. Lord Dreever might be hounded into
proposing to Molly, but what earthly reason was there
for supposing that Molly would accept him? He
declined even for an instant to look upon Spennie's

title in the light of a lure. Molly was not the girl to marry for a title. He endeavored to examine impartially his lordship's other claims. He was a pleasant fellow, with - to judge on short acquaintanceship - an undeniably amiable disposition. That much must be conceded. But against this must be placed the equally undeniable fact that he was also, as he would have put it himself, a most frightful ass. He was weak. Pie had no character. Altogether, the examination made Jimmy more cheerful. He could not see the light-haired one, even with Sir Thomas Blunt shoving behind, as it were, accomplishing the knight's ends. Shove he never so wisely, Sir Thomas could never make a Romeo out of Spennie Dreever.

It was while sitting in the billiard-room one night after dinner, watching his rival play a hundred up with the silent Hargate, that Jimmy came definitely to this conclusion. He had stopped there to watch, more because he wished to study his man at close range than because the game was anything out of the common as an exposition of billiards. As a matter of fact, it would have been hard to imagine a worse game. Lord Dreever, who was conceding twenty, was poor, and his opponent an obvious beginner. Again, as he looked on, Jimmy was possessed of an idea that he had met Hargate before. But, once more, he searched his memory, and drew blank. He did not give the thing much thought, being intent on his diagnosis of Lord Dreever, who by a fluky series of cannons had wobbled into the forties, and was now a few points ahead of his opponent.

Presently, having summed his lordship up to his satisfaction and grown bored with the game, Jimmy strolled out of the room. He paused outside the door for a moment, wondering what to do. There was bridge in the smoking-room, but he did not feel inclined for bridge. From the drawing-room came sounds of music. He turned in that direction, then stopped again. He came to the conclusion that he did not feel sociable. He wanted to think. A cigar on the terrace would meet his needs.

He went up to his room for his cigar-case. The window was open. He leaned out. There was almost a full moon, and it was very light out of doors. His eye was caught by a movement at the further end of the terrace, where the shadow was. A girl came out of the shadow, walking slowly.

Not since early boyhood had Jimmy descended stairs with such a rare burst of speed. He negotiated the nasty turn at the end of the first flight at quite a suicidal pace. Fate, however, had apparently wakened again and resumed business, for he did not break his neck. A few moments later, he was out on the terrace, bearing a cloak which, he had snatched up en route in the hall.

"I thought you might be cold," he said, breathing quickly.

"Oh, thank you," said Molly. "How kind of you!" He put it round her shoulders. "Have you. been running?"

"I came downstairs rather fast."

"Were you afraid the boogaboos would get you?" she laughed. "I was thinking of when I was a small child. I was always afraid of them. I used, to race downstairs when I had to go to my room in the dark, unless I could persuade someone to hold my hand all the way there and back."

Her spirits had risen with Jimmy's arrival. Things had been happening that worried her. She had gone out on to the terrace to be alone. When she heard his footsteps, she had dreaded the advent of some garrulous fellow-guest, full of small talk. Jimmy, somehow, was a comfort. He did not disturb the atmosphere. Little as they had seen of each other, something in him - she could not say what - had drawn her to him. He was a man whom she could trust instinctively.

They walked on in silence. Words were pouring into Jimmy's mind, but he could not frame them. He seemed to have lost the power of coherent thought.

Molly said nothing. It was not a night for conversation. The moon had turned terrace and garden into a fairyland of black and silver. It was a night to look and listen and think.

They walked slowly up and down. As they turned for the second time, Molly's thoughts formed themselves into a question. Twice she was on the point of asking it, but each time she checked herself. It was an impossible question. She had no right to put it, and he had no right to answer. Yet, something was driving her on to ask it.

It came out suddenly, without warning.

"Mr. Pitt, what do you think of Lord Dreever?"

Jimmy started. No question could have chimed in more aptly with his thoughts. Even as she spoke, he was struggling to keep himself from asking her the same thing.

"Oh, I know I ought not to ask," she went on. "He's your host, and you're his friend. I know. But - "

Her voice trailed off. The muscles of Jimmy's back tightened and quivered. But he could find no words.

"I wouldn't ask anyone else. But you're - different, somehow. I don't know what I mean. We hardly know each other. But - "

She stopped again; and still he was dumb.

"I feel so alone," she said very quietly, almost to herself. Something seemed to break in Jimmy's head. His brain suddenly cleared. He took a step forward.

A huge shadow blackened the white grass. Jimmy wheeled round. It was McEachern.

"I have been looking for you, Molly, my dear," he said, heavily. "I thought you must have gone to bed."

He turned to Jimmy, and addressed him for the first time since their meeting in the bedroom.

"Will you excuse us, Mr. Pitt?"

Jimmy bowed, and walked rapidly toward the house. At the door, he stopped and looked back. The two were standing where he had left them.

CHAPTER XVI

A MARRIAGE ARRANGED

Neither Molly nor her father had moved or spoken while Jimmy was covering the short strip of turf that ended at the stone steps of the house. McEachern stood looking down at her in grim silence. His great body against the dark mass of the castle wall seemed larger than ever in the uncertain light. To Molly, there was something sinister and menacing in his attitude. She found herself longing that Jimmy would come back. She was frightened. Why, she could not have said. It was as if some instinct told her that a crisis in her affairs had been reached, and that she needed him. For the first time in her life, she felt nervous in her father's company. Ever since she was a child, she had been accustomed to look upon him as her protector; hut, now, she was afraid.

"Father!" she cried.

"What are you doing out here?"

His voice was tense and strained.

"I came out because I wanted to think, father, dear."

She thought she knew his moods, but this was one that

she had never seen. It frightened her.

"Why did he come out here?"

"Mr. Pitt? He brought me a wrap."

"What was he saying to you?"

The rain of questions gave Molly a sensation of being battered. She felt dazed, and a little mutinous. What had she done that she should be assailed like this?

"He was saying nothing," she said, rather shortly.

"Nothing? What do you mean? What was he saying? Tell me!"

Molly's voice shook as she replied.

"He was saying nothing," she repeated. "Do you think I'm not telling the truth, father? He had not spoken a word for ever so long. We just walked up and down. I was thinking, and I suppose he was, too. At any rate, he said nothing. I - I think you might believe me."

She began to cry quietly. Her father had never been like this before. It hurt her.

McEachern's manner changed in a flash. In the shock of finding Jimmy and Molly together on the terrace, he had forgotten himself. He had had reason, to be suspicious. Sir Thomas Blunt, from whom he had just parted, had told him a certain piece of news which had disturbed him. The discovery of Jimmy with Molly had lent an added significance to that piece of news. He saw that he had been rough. In a moment, he was by her side, his great arm round her shoulder, petting and comforting her as he had done when she was a child. He believed her word without question; and his relief made him very tender. Gradually, the sobs ceased. She leaned against his arm.

"I'm tired, father," she whispered.

"Poor little girl. We'll sit down."

There was a seat at the end of the terrace. McEachern picked Molly up as if she had been a baby, and carried her to it. She gave a little cry.

"I didn't mean I was too tired to walk," she said, laughing tremulously. "How strong you are, father! If I was naughty, you could take me up and shake me till I was good, couldn't you?"

"Of course. And send you to bed, too. So, you, be careful, young woman."

He lowered her to the seat. Molly drew the cloak closer round her, and shivered.

"Cold, dear?"

"No."

"You shivered."

"It was nothing. Yes, it was," she went on quickly; "it was. Father, will you promise me something?"

"Of course. What?"

"Don't ever be angry with me like that again, will you? I couldn't bear it. Really, I couldn't. I know it's stupid of me, but it hurt. You don't know how it hurt."

"But, my dear - "

"Oh, I know it's stupid. But - "

"But, my darling, it wasn't so. I was angry, but it wasn't with you."

"With - ? Were you angry with Mr. Pitt?"

McEachern saw that he had traveled too far. He had intended that Jimmy's existence should be forgotten for the time being. He had other things to discuss. But it was too late now. He must go forward.

"I didn't like to see you out here alone with Mr. Pitt, dear," he said. "I was afraid - "

He saw that he must go still further forward. It was more than, awkward. He wished to hint at the undesirability of an entanglement with Jimmy without admitting the possibility of it. Not being a man, of nimble brain, he found this somewhat beyond his powers.

"I don't like him," he said, briefly. "He's crooked."

Molly's eyes opened wide. The color had gone from her face.

"Crooked, father?"

McEachern perceived that he had traveled very much

too far, almost to disaster. He longed to denounce Jimmy, but he was gagged. If Molly were to ask the question, that Jimmy had asked in the bedroom - that fatal, unanswerable question! The price was too great to pay.

He spoke cautiously, vaguely, feeling his way.

"I couldn't explain to you, my dear. You wouldn't understand. You must remember, my dear, that out in New York I was in a position to know a great many queer characters - crooks, Molly. I was working among them."

"But, father, that night at our house you didn't know Mr. Pitt. He had to tell you his name."

"I didn't know him - then," said her father slowly, "but - but - " he paused - "but I made inquiries," he concluded with a rush, "and found out things."

He permitted himself a long, silent breath of relief. He saw his way now.

"Inquiries?" said Molly. "Why?"

"Why?"

"Why did you suspect him?"

A moment earlier, the question might have confused McEachern, but not now. He was equal to it. He took it in his stride.

"It's hard to say. my dear, A man who has had as much to do with crooks as I have recognizes them when he sees them."

"Did you think Mr. Pitt looked - looked like that?" Her voice was very small. There was a drawn, pinched expression on her face. She was paler than ever.

He could not divine her thoughts. He could not know what his words had done; how they had shown her in a flash what Jimmy was to her, and lighted her mind like a flame, revealing the secret hidden there. She knew now. The feeling of comradeship, the instinctive trust, the sense of dependence - they no longer perplexed her; they were signs which she could read.

And he was crooked!

McEachern proceeded. Belief made him buoyant.

"I did, my dear. I can read them like a book. I've met scores of his sort. Broadway is full of them. Good clothes and a pleasant manner don't make a man honest. I've run up against a mighty high-toned bunch of crooks in my day. It's a long time since I gave up thinking that it was only the ones with the low foreheads and the thick ears that needed watching. It's the innocent Willies who look as if all they could do was to lead the cotillon. This man Pitt's one of them. I'm not guessing, mind you. I know. I know his line, and all about him. I'm watching him. He's here on some game. How did he get here? Why, he scraped acquaintance with Lord Dreever in a London restaurant. It's the commonest trick on the list. If I hadn't happened to be here when he came, I suppose he'd have made his haul by now. Why, he came all prepared for it! Have you seen an ugly, grinning, red-headed scoundrel hanging about the place? His valet.

So he says. Valet! Do you know who that is? That's one of the most notorious yegg-men on the other side. There isn't a policeman in New York who doesn't know Spike Mullins. Even if I knew nothing of this Pitt, that would be enough. What's an innocent man going round the country with Spike Mullins for, unless they are standing in together at some game? That's who Mr. Pitt is, my dear, and that's why maybe I seemed a little put out when I came upon you and him out here alone together. See as little of him as you can. In a large party like this, it won't be difficult to avoid him."

Molly sat staring out across the garden. At first, every word had been a stab. Several times, she had been on the point of crying out that she could bear it no longer. But, gradually, a numbness succeeded the pain. She found herself listening apathetically.

McEachern talked on. He left the subject of Jimmy, comfortably conscious that, even if there had ever existed in Molly's heart any budding feeling of the kind he had suspected, it must now be dead. He steered the conversation away until it ran easily among commonplaces. He talked of New York, of the preparations for the theatricals. Molly answered composedly. She was still pale, and a certain listlessness in her manner might have been noticed by a more observant man than Mr. McEachern. Beyond this, there was nothing to show that her heart had been born and killed but a few minutes before. Women have the Red Indian instinct; and Molly had grown to womanhood in those few minutes.

Presently, Lord Dreever's name came up. It caused a momentary pause, and McEachern took advantage of it. It was the cue for which he had been waiting. He hesitated for a moment, for the conversation was about to enter upon a difficult phase, and he was not quite sure of himself. Then, he took the plunge.

"I have just been talking to Sir Thomas, my dear," he said. He tried to speak casually, and, as a natural result, infused so much meaning into his voice that Molly looked at him in surprise. McEachern coughed confusedly. Diplomacy, he concluded, was not his forte. He abandoned it in favor of directness. "He was telling me that you had refused Lord Dreever this evening."

"Yes. I did," said Molly. "How did Sir Thomas know?"

"Lord Dreever told him."

Molly raised her eyebrows.

"I shouldn't have thought it was the sort of thing he would talk about," she said.

"Sir Thomas is his uncle."

"Of course, so he is," said Molly, dryly. "I forgot. That would account for it, wouldn't it?"

Mr. McEachern looked at her with some concern. There was a hard ring in her voice which he did not altogether like. His greatest admirer had never called him an intuitive man, and he was quite at a loss to see what was wrong. As a schemer, he was perhaps a little naive. He had taken it for granted that Molly was ignorant of the maneuvers which had been going on, and which had culminated that afternoon in a stammering proposal of marriage from Lord Dreever in the rose-garden. This, however, was not the case. The woman incapable of seeing through the machinations of two men of the mental caliber of Sir Thomas Blunt and Mr. McEachern has yet to be born. For some considerable time, Molly had been alive to the well-meant plottings of that worthy pair, and had derived little pleasure from the fact. It may be that woman loves to be pursued; but she does not love to be pursued by a crowd.

Mr. McEachern cleared his throat, and began again.

"You shouldn't decide a question like that too hastily, my dear."

"I didn't - not too hastily for Lord Dreever, at any rate, poor dear."

"It was in your power," said Mr. McEachern portentously, "to make a man happy - "

"I did," said Molly, bitterly. "You should have seen his face light up. He could hardly believe it was true for a moment, and then it came home to him, and I thought he would have fallen on my neck. He did his very best to look heart-broken - out of politeness - but it was no good. He whistled most of the way back to the house – all flat, but very cheerfully."

"My dear! What do you mean?"

Molly had made the discovery earlier in their conversation that her father had moods whose existence she had not expected. It was his turn now to make a similar discovery regarding herself.

"I mean nothing, father," she said. "I'm just telling you what happened. He came to me looking like a dog that's going to be washed - "

"Why, of course, he was nervous, my dear."

"Of course. He couldn't know that I was going to refuse him."

She was breathing quickly. He started to speak, but she went on, looking straight before her. Her face was very white in the moon-light.

"He took me into the rose-garden. Was that Sir Thomas's idea? There couldn't have been a better setting, I'm sure. The roses looked lovely. Presently, I heard him gulp, and I was so sorry for him I I would have refused him then, and put him out of his misery, only I couldn't very well till he had proposed, could I? So, I turned my back, and sniffed at a rose. And, then, he shut his eyes - I couldn't see him, but I know he shut his eyes - and began to say his lesson."

"Molly!"

She laughed, hysterically.

"He did. He said his lesson. He gabbled it. When he had got as far as, 'Well, don't you know, what I mean is, that's what I wanted to say, you know,' I turned round and soothed him. I said I didn't love him. He said, 'No, no, of course not.' I said he had paid me a great compliment. He said, 'Not at all,' looking very anxious, poor darling, as if even then he was afraid of what might come next. But I reassured him, and he cheered up, and we walked back to the house together, as happy as could be."

McEachern put his hand round her shoulders. She winced, but let it stay. He attempted gruff conciliation.

"My dear, you've been imagining things. Of course, he isn't happy. Why, I saw the young fellow - "

Recollecting that the last time he had seen the young fellow - shortly after dinner - the young fellow had been occupied in juggling, with every appearance of mental peace, two billiard-balls and a box of matches, he broke off abruptly.

Molly looked at him.

"Father."

"My dear?"

"Why do you want me to marry Lord Dreever?"

He met the attack stoutly.

"I think he's a fine young fellow," he said, avoiding her eyes.

"He's quite nice," said Molly, quietly.

McEachern had been trying not to say it. He did not wish to say it. If it could have been hinted at, he would have done it. But he was not good at hinting. A lifetime passed in surroundings where the subtlest hint is a drive in the ribs with a truncheon does not leave a man an adept at the art. He had to be blunt or silent.

"He's the Earl of Dreever, my dear."

He rushed on, desperately anxious to cover the nakedness of the statement in a comfortable garment of words.

"Why, you see, you're young, Molly. It's only natural you shouldn't look on these things sensibly. You expect too much of a man. You expect this young fellow to be like the heroes of the novels you read. When you've lived a little longer, my dear, you'll see that there's nothing in it. It isn't the hero of the novel you want to marry. It's the man who'll make you a good husband."

This remark struck Mr. McEachern as so pithy and profound that he repeated it.

He went on. Molly was sitting quite still, looking into the shrubbery. He assumed she was listening; but whether she was or not, he must go on talking. The situation was difficult. Silence would make it more difficult.

"Now, look at Lord Dreever," he said. "There's a young man with one of the oldest titles in England. He could go anywhere and do what he liked, and be excused for whatever he did because of his name. But he doesn't. He's got the right stuff in him. He doesn't go racketing around - "

"His uncle doesn't allow him enough pocket-money," said Molly, with a jarring little laugh. "Perhaps, that's why."

There was a pause. McEachern required a few

moments in which to marshal his arguments once more. He had been thrown out of his stride.

Molly turned to him. The hardness had gone from her face. She looked up at him wistfully.

"Father, dear, listen," she said. "We always used to understand each other so well!" He patted her shoulder affectionately. "You can't mean what you say? You know I don't love Lord Dreever. You know he's only a boy. Don't you want me to marry a man? I love this old place, but surely you can't think that it can really matter in a thing like this? You don't really mean, that about the hero of the novel? I'm not stupid, like that. I only want - oh, I can't put it into words, but don't you see?"

Her eyes were fixed appealingly on him. It only needed a word from him - perhaps not even a word - to close the gulf that had opened between them.

He missed the chance. He had had time to think, and his arguments were ready again. With stolid good-humor, he marched along the line he had mapped out. He was kindly and shrewd and practical; and the gulf gaped wider with every word.

"You mustn't be rash, my dear. You mustn't act without thinking in these things. Lord Dreever is only a boy, as you say, but he will grow. You say you don't love him. Nonsense! You like him. You would go on liking him more and more. And why? Because you could make what you pleased of him. You've got character, my dear. With a girl like you to look after him, he would go a long way, a very long way. It's all there. It only wants bringing out. And think of it,

Molly! Countess of Dreever! There's hardly a better title in England. It would make me very happy, my dear. It's been my one hope all these years to see you in the place where you ought to be. And now the chance has come. Molly, dear, don't throw it away."

She had leaned back with closed eyes. A wave of exhaustion had swept over her. She listened in a dull dream. She felt beaten. They were too strong for her. There were too many of them. What did it matter? Why not give in, and end it all and win peace? That was all she wanted - peace now. What did it all matter?

"Very well, father," she said, listlessly.

McEachern stopped short.

"You'll do it, dear?" he cried. "You will?"

"Very well, father."

He stooped and kissed her.

"My own dear little girl," he said.

She got up.

"I'm rather tired, father," she said. "I think I'll go in."

Two minutes later, Mr. McEachern was in Sir Thomas Blunt's study. Five minutes later, Sir Thomas pressed the bell.

Saunders appeared.

"Tell his lordship," said Sir Thomas, "that I wish to see him a moment. He is in the billiard-room, I think."

CHAPTER XVII

JIMMY REMEMBERS SOMETHING

The game between Hargate and Lord Dreever was still in progress when Jimmy returned to the billiard-room. A glance at the board showed that the score was seventy - sixty-nine, in favor of spot.

"Good game," said Jimmy. "Who's spot?"

"I am," said his lordship, missing an easy cannon. For some reason, he appeared in high spirits. "Hargate's been going great guns. I was eleven ahead a moment ago, but he made a break of twelve."

Lord Dreever belonged to the class of billiard-players to whom a double-figure break is a thing to be noted and greeted with respect.

"Fluky," muttered the silent Hargate, deprecatingly. This was a long speech for him. Since their meeting at Paddington station, Jimmy had seldom heard him utter anything beyond a monosyllable.

"Not a bit of it, dear old son," said Lord Dreever, handsomely. "You're coming on like a two-year-old. I sha'n't be able to give you twenty in a hundred much longer."

He went to a side-table, and mixed himself a whiskey-and-soda, singing a brief extract from musical comedy as he did so. There could be no shadow of doubt that he was finding life good. For the past few days, and particularly that afternoon, he had been rather noticeably ill at ease. Jimmy had seen him hanging about the terrace at half-past five, and had thought that he looked like a mute at a funeral. But now, only a few hours later, he was beaming on the world, and chirping like a bird.

The game moved jerkily along. Jimmy took a seat, and watched. The score mounted slowly. Lord Dreever was bad, but Hargate was worse. At length, in the eighties, his lordship struck a brilliant vein. When he had finished his break, his score was ninety-five. Hargate, who had profited by a series of misses on his opponent's part, had reached ninety-six.

"This is shortening my life," said Jimmy, leaning forward.

The balls had been left in an ideal position. Even Hargate could not fail to make a cannon. He made it.

A close finish to even the worst game is exciting. Jimmy leaned still further forward to watch the next stroke. It looked as if Hargate would have to wait for his victory. A good player could have made a cannon as the balls lay, but not Hargate. They were almost in a straight line, with, white in the center.

Hargate swore under his breath. There was nothing to be done. He struck carelessly at white. White rolled against red, seemed to hang for a moment, and shot straight back against spot. The game was over.

"Great Scott! What a fluke!" cried the silent one, becoming quite garrulous at the miracle.

A quiet grin spread itself slowly across Jimmy's face. He had remembered what he had been trying to remember for over a week.

At this moment, the door opened, and Saunders appeared. "Sir Thomas would like to see your lordship in his study," he said.

"Eh? What does he want?"

"Sir Thomas did not confide in me, your lordship."

"Eh? What? Oh, no! Well, see you later, you men."

He rested his cue against the table, and put on his coat. Jimmy followed him out of the door, which he shut behind him.

"One second, Dreever," he said.

"Eh? Hullo! What's up?"

"Any money on that game?" asked Jimmy.

"Why, yes, by Jove, now you mention it, there was. An even fiver. And - er - by the way, old man - the fact is, just for the moment, I'm frightfully - You haven't such a thing as a fiver anywhere about, have you? The fact is - "

"My dear fellow, of course. I'll square up with him now, shall I?"

"Fearfully obliged, if you would. Thanks, old man. Pay it to-morrow."

"No hurry," said Jimmy; "plenty more in the old oak chest."

He went back to the room. Hargate was practising cannons. He was on the point of making a stroke when Jimmy opened the door.

"Care for a game?" said Hargate.

"Not just at present," said Jimmy.

Hargate attempted his cannon, and failed badly. Jimmy smiled.

"Not such a good shot as the last," he said.

"No."

"Fine shot, that other."

"Fluke."

"I wonder."

Jimmy lighted a cigarette.

"Do you know New York at all?" he asked.

"Been there."

"Ever been in the Strollers' Club?"

Hargate turned his back, but Jimmy had seen his face,

and was satisfied.

"Don't know it," said Hargate.

"Great place," said Jimmy. "Mostly actors and writers, and so on. The only drawback is that some of them pick up queer friends."

Hargate did not reply. He did not seem interested.

"Yes," went on Jimmy. "For instance, a pal of mine, an actor named Mifflin, introduced a man a year ago as a member's guest for a fortnight, and this man rooked the fellows of I don't know how much at billiards. The old game, you know. Nursing his man right up to the end, and then finishing with a burst. Of course, when that happens once or twice, it may be an accident, but, when a man who poses as a novice always manages by a really brilliant shot - "

Hargate turned round.

"They fired this fellow out," said Jimmy.

"Look here!"

"Yes?"

"What do you mean?"

"It's a dull yarn," said Jimmy, apologetically. "I've been boring you. By the way, Dreever asked me to square up with you for that game, in case he shouldn't be back. Here you are."

He held out an empty hand.

"Got it?"

"What are you going to do?" demanded Hargate.

"What am I going to do?" queried Jimmy.

"You know what I mean. If you'll keep your mouth shut, and stand in, it's halves. Is that what you're after?"

Jimmy was delighted. He knew that by rights the proposal should have brought him from his seat, with stern, set face, to wreak vengeance for the insult, but on such occasions he was apt to ignore the conventions. His impulse, when he met a man whose code of behavior was not the ordinary code, was to chat with him and extract his point of view. He felt as little animus against Hargate as he had felt against Spike on the occasion of their first meeting.

"Do you make much at this sort of game?" he asked.

Hargate was relieved. This was business-like.

"Pots," he said, with some enthusiasm. "Pots. I tell you, if you'll stand in - "

"Bit risky, isn't it?"

"Not a bit of it. An occasional accident - "

"I suppose you'd call me one?"

Hargate grinned.

"It must be pretty tough work," said Jimmy. "You must

have to use a tremendous lot of self-restraint."

Hargate sighed.

"That's the worst of it," he admitted, "the having to seem a mug at the game. I've been patronized sometimes by young fools, who thought they were teaching me, till I nearly forgot myself and showed them what real billiards was."

"There's always some drawback to the learned professions," said Jimmy.

"But there's a heap to make up for it in this one," said Hargate. "Well, look here, is it a deal? You'll stand in - "

Jimmy shook his head.

"I guess not," he said. "It's good of you, but commercial speculation never was in my line. I'm afraid you must count me out of this."

"What! You're going to tell - ?"

"No," said Jimmy, "I'm not. I'm not a vigilance committee. I won't
tell a soul."

"'Why, then - " began Hargate, relieved.

"Unless, of course," Jimmy went on, "you play billiards again while you're here."

Hargate stared.

"But, damn it, man, if I don't, what's the good - ? Look here. What am I to do if they ask me to play?"

"Give your wrist as an excuse."

"My wrist?"

"Yes. You sprained it to-morrow after breakfast. It was bad luck. I wonder how you came to do it. You didn't sprain it much, but just enough to stop you playing billiards."

Hargate reflected.

"Understand?" said Jimmy.

"Oh, very well," said Hargate, sullenly. "But," he burst out, "if I ever get a chance to get even with you - "

"You won't," said Jimmy. "Dismiss the rosy dream. Get even! You don't know me. There's not a flaw in my armor. I'm a sort of modern edition of the stainless knight. Tennyson drew Galahad from me. I move through life with almost a sickening absence of sin. But hush! We are observed. At least, we shall be in another minute. Somebody is coming down the passage. You do understand, don't you? Sprained wrist is the watchword."

The handle turned. It was Lord Dreever, back again, from his interview.

"Hullo, Dreever," said Jimmy. "We've missed you. Hargate has been doing his best to amuse me with acrobatic tricks. But you're too reckless, Hargate, old man. Mark my words, one of these days you'll be spraining your wrist. You should be more careful. What, going? Good-night. Pleasant fellow, Hargate," he added, as the footsteps retreated down, the passage. "Well, my lad, what's the matter with you? You look depressed."

Lord Dreever flung himself on to the lounge, and groaned hollowly.

"Damn! Damn!! Damn.!!!" he observed.

His glassy eye met Jimmy's, and wandered away again.

"What on earth's the matter?" demanded Jimmy. "You go out of here caroling like a song-bird, and you come back moaning like a lost soul. What's happened?"

"Give me a brandy-and-soda, Pitt, old man. There's a good chap. I'm in a fearful hole."

"Why? What's the matter?"

"I'm engaged," groaned his lordship.

"Engaged! I wish you'd explain. What on earth's wrong with you? Don't you want to be engaged? What's your - ?"

He broke off, as a sudden, awful suspicion dawned upon him. "Who is she?" he cried.

He gripped the stricken peer's shoulder, and shook it savagely. Unfortunately, he selected the precise moment when the latter was in the act of calming his quivering nerve-centers with a gulp of brandy-and-soda, and for the space of some two minutes it seemed as if the engagement would be broken off by the premature extinction of the Dreever line. A long and painful fit of coughing, however, ended with his lordship still alive and on the road to recovery.

He eyed Jimmy reproachfully, but Jimmy was in no mood for apologies.

"Who is she?" he kept demanding. "What's her name?"

"Might have killed me!" grumbled the convalescent.

"Who is she?"

"What? Why, Miss McEachern."

Jimmy had known what the answer would be, but it was scarcely less of a shock for that reason.

"Miss McEachern?" he echoed.

Lord Dreever nodded a somber nod.

"You're engaged to her?"

Another somber nod.

"I don't believe it," said Jimmy.

"I wish I didn't," said his lordship wistfully, ignoring the slight rudeness of the remark. "But, worse luck, it's true."

For the first time since the disclosure of the name, Jimmy's attention was directed to the remarkable demeanor of his successful rival.

"You don't seem over-pleased," he said.

"Pleased! Have a fiver each way on 'pleased'! No, I'm not exactly leaping with joy."

"Then, what the devil is it all about? What do you mean? What's the idea? If you don't want to marry Miss McEachern, why did you propose to her?"

Lord Dreever closed his eyes.

"Dear old boy, don't! It's my uncle."

"Your uncle?"

"Didn't I explain it all to you - about him wanting me to marry? You know! I told you the whole thing."

Jimmy stared in silence.

"Do you mean to say - ?" he said, slowly.

He stopped. It was a profanation to put the thing into words.

"What, old man?"

Jimmy gulped.

"Do you mean to say you want to marry Miss McEachern simply because she has money?" he said.

It was not the first time that he had heard of a case of a British peer marrying for such a reason, but it was the first time that the thing had filled him with horror. In some circumstances, things come home more forcibly to us.

"It's not me, old man," murmured his lordship; "it's my uncle."

"Your uncle! Good God!" Jimmy clenched his hands, despairingly. "Do you mean to say that you let your uncle order you about in a thing like this? Do you mean to say you're such a - such a - such a gelatine - backboneless worm - "

"Old man! I say!" protested his lordship, wounded.

"I'd call you a wretched knock-kneed skunk, only I don't want to be fulsome. I hate flattering a man to his face."

Lord Dreever, deeply pained, half-rose from his seat.

"Don't get up," urged Jimmy, smoothly. "I couldn't trust myself." His lordship subsided hastily. He was feeling alarmed. He had never seen this side of Jimmy's character. At first, he had been merely aggrieved and disappointed. He had expected sympathy. How, the matter had become more serious. Jimmy was pacing the room like a young and hungry tiger. At present, it was true, there was a billiard-table between them; but his lordship felt that he could have done with good, stout bars. He nestled in his seat with the earnest concentration of a limpet on a rock. It would be deuced bad form, of course, for Jimmy to assault his host, but could Jimmy be trusted to remember the niceties of etiquette?

"Why the devil she accepted you, I can't think," said

Jimmy half to himself, stopping suddenly, and glaring across the table.

Lord Dreever felt relieved. This was not polite, perhaps, but at least it was not violent.

"That's what beats me, too, old man," he said.

"Between you and me, it's a jolly rum business. This afternoon - "

"What about this afternoon?"

"Why, she wouldn't have me at any price."

"You asked her this afternoon?"

"Yes, and it was all right then. She refused me like a bird. Wouldn't hear of it. Came damn near laughing in my face. And then, to-night," he went on, his voice squeaky at the thought of his wrongs, "my uncle sends for me, and says she's changed her mind and is waiting for me in the morning-room. I go there, and she tells me in about three words that she's been thinking it over and that the whole fearful thing is on again. I call it jolly rough on a chap. I felt such a frightful ass, you know. I didn't know what to do, whether to kiss her, I mean - "

Jimmy snorted violently.

"Eh?" said his lordship, blankly.

"Go on," said Jimmy, between his teeth.

"I felt a fearful fool, you know. I just said 'Right ho!' or something - dashed if I know now what I did say - and legged it. It's a jolly rum business, the whole thing. It isn't as if she wanted me. I could see that with half an eye. She doesn't care a hang for me. It's my belief, old man," he said solemnly, "that she's been badgered into it, I believe my uncle's been at her."

Jimmy laughed shortly.

"My dear man, you seem to think your uncle's persuasive influence is universal. I guess it's confined to you."

"Well, anyhow, I believe that's what's happened. What do you say?"

"Why say anything? There doesn't seem to be much need."

He poured some brandy into a glass, and added a little soda.

"You take it pretty stiff," observed his lordship, with a touch of envy.

"On occasion," said Jimmy, emptying the glass.

CHAPTER XVIII

THE LOCHINVAR METHOD

As Jimmy sat smoking a last cigarette in his bedroom before going to bed that night, Spike Mullins came in. Jimmy had been thinking things over. He was one of those men who are at their best in a losing game. Imminent disaster always had the effect of keying him up and putting an edge on his mind. The news he had heard that night had left him with undiminished determination, but conscious that a change of method would be needed. He must stake all on a single throw now. Young Lochinvar rather than Romeo must be his model. He declined to believe himself incapable of getting anything that he wanted as badly as he wanted Molly. He also declined to believe that she was really attached to Lord Dreever. He suspected the hand of McEachern in the affair, though the suspicion did not clear up the mystery by any means. Molly was a girl of character, not a feminine counterpart of his lordship, content meekly to do what she was told in a matter of this kind. The whole thing puzzled him.

"Well, Spike?" he said.

He was not too pleased at the interruption. He was thinking, and he wanted to be alone.

Something appeared to have disturbed Spike. His

bearing was excited.

"Say, boss! Guess what. You know dat guy dat come dis afternoon - de guy from de village, dat came wit' old man McEachern?"

"Galer?" said Jimmy. "What about him?"

There had been an addition to the guests at the castle that afternoon. Mr. McEachern, walking in the village, had happened upon an old New York acquaintance of his, who, touring England, had reached Dreever and was anxious to see the historic castle. Mr. McEachern had brought him thither, introduced him to Sir Thomas, and now Mr. Samuel Galer was occupying a room on the same floor as Jimmy's. He had appeared at dinner that night, a short, wooden-faced man, with no more conversation than Hargate. Jimmy had paid little attention to the newcomer.

"What about him?" he said.

"He's a sleut', boss."

"A what?"

"A sleut'."

"A detective?"

"Dat's right. A fly cop."

"What makes you think that?"

"T'ink! Why, I can tell dem by deir eyes an' deir feet, an' de whole of dem. I could pick out a fly cop from a bunch of a t'ousand. He's a sure 'nough sleut' all right, all right. I seen him rubber in' at youse, boss."

"At me! Why at me? Why, of course. I see now. Our friend McEachern has got him in to spy on us."

"Dat's right, boss."

"Of course, you may be mistaken."

"Not me, boss. An', say, he ain't de only one."

"What, more detectives? They'll have to put up 'House Full' boards, at this rate. Who's the other?"

"A mug what's down in de soivants' hall. I wasn't so sure of him at foist, but now I'm onto his curves. He's a sleut' all right. He's vally to Sir Tummas, dis second mug is. But he ain't no vally. He's come to see no one don't get busy wit' de jools. Say, what do youse t'ink of dem jools, boss?"

"Finest I ever saw."

"Yes, dat's right. A hundred t'ousand plunks dey set him back. Dey're de limit, ain't dey? Say, won't youse really - ?"

"Spike! I'm surprised at you! Do you know, you're getting a regular Mephistopheles, Spike? Suppose I hadn't an iron will, what would happen? You really must select your subjects of conversation more carefully. You're bad company for the likes of me."

Spike shuffled despondently.

"But, boss - !"

Jimmy shook his head.

"It can't be done, my lad."

"But it can, boss," protested Spike. "It's dead easy. I've been up to de room, an' I seen de box what de jools is kept in. Why, it's de softest ever! We could get dem as easy as pullin' de plug out of a bottle. Why, say, dere's never been such a peach of a place for gittin' hold of de stuff as dis house. Dat's right, boss. Why, look what I got dis afternoon, just snoopin' around an' not really tryin' to git busy at all. It was just lyin' about."

He plunged his hand into his pocket, and drew it out again. As he unclosed his fingers, Jimmy caught the gleam of precious stones.

"What the - !" he gasped.

Spike was looking at his treasure-trove with an air of affectionate proprietorship.

"Where on earth did you get those?" asked Jimmy.

"Out of one of de rooms. Dey belonged to one of de loidies. It was de easiest old t'ing ever, boss. I just went in when dere was nobody around, an' dere dey was on de toible. I never butted into anyt'in' so soft."

"Spike!"

"Yes, boss?"

"Do you remember the room you took them from?"

"Sure. It was de foist on de - "

"Then, just listen to me for a moment, my bright boy. When we're at breakfast to-morrow, you want to go to that room and put those things back - all of them, mind you - just where you found them. Do you understand?"

Spike's jaw had fallen.

"Put dem back, boss!" he faltered.

"Every single one of them."

"Boss!" said Spike, plaintively.

"Remember. Every single one of them, just where it belongs. See?"

"Very well, boss."

The dejection in his voice would have moved the sternest to pity. Gloom had enveloped Spike's spirit. The sunlight had gone out of his life.

It had also gone out of the lives of a good many other people at the castle. This was mainly due to the growing shadow of the day of the theatricals.

For pure discomfort, there are few things in the world that can compete with the final rehearsals of an amateur theatrical performance at a country-house. Every day, the atmosphere becomes more heavily charged with restlessness and depression. The producer of the piece, especially if he be also the author of it, develops a sort of intermittent insanity. He plucks at his mustache, if he has one: at his hair, if he has not.

He mutters to himself. He gives vent to occasional despairing cries. The soothing suavity that marked his demeanor in the earlier rehearsals disappears. He no longer says with a winning smile, "Splendid, old man, splendid. Couldn't be better. But I think we'll take that over just once more, if you don't mind." Instead, he rolls his eyes, and snaps out, "Once more, please. This'll never do. At this rate, we might just as well cut out the show altogether. What's that? No, it won't be all right on the night! Now, then, once more; and do pull yourselves together this time." After this, the scene is sulkily resumed; and conversation, when the parties concerned meet subsequently, is cold and strained.

Matters had reached this stage at the castle. Everybody was thoroughly tired of the piece, and, but for the thought of the disappointment which (presumably) would rack the neighboring nobility and gentry if it were not to be produced, would have resigned their places without a twinge of regret. People who had schemed to get the best and longest parts were wishing now that they had been content with "First Footman," or "Giles, a villager."

"I'll never run an amateur show again as long as I live," confided Charteris to Jimmy almost tearfully. "It's not good enough. Most of them aren't word-perfect yet."

"It'll be all right - "

"Oh, don't say it'll be all right on the night."

"I wasn't going to," said Jimmy. "I was going to say it'll be all right after the night. People will soon forget how badly the thing went."

"You're a nice, comforting sort of man, aren't you?" said Charteris.

"Why worry?" said Jimmy. "If you go on like this, it'll be Westminster Abbey for you in your prime. You'll be getting brain-fever."

Jimmy himself was one of the few who were feeling reasonably cheerful. He was deriving a keen amusement at present from the maneuvers of Mr. Samuel Galer, of New York. This lynx-eyed man; having been instructed by Mr. McEachern to watch Jimmy, was doing so with a thoroughness that would have roused the suspicions of a babe. If Jimmy went to the billiard-room after dinner, Mr. Galer was there to keep him company. If, during the course of the day, he had occasion to fetch a handkerchief or a cigarette-case from his bedroom, he was sure, on emerging, to stumble upon Mr. Galer in the corridor. The employees of Dodson's Private Inquiry Agency believed in earning their salaries.

Occasionally, after these encounters, Jimmy would come upon Sir Thomas Blunt's valet, the other man in whom Spike's trained eye had discerned the distinguishing marks of the sleuth. He was usually somewhere round the corner at these moments, and, when collided with, apologized with great politeness. Jimmy decided that he must have come under suspicion in this case vicariously, through Spike. Spike in the servants' hall would, of course, stand out conspicuously enough to catch the eye of a detective on the look out for sin among the servants; and he himself, as Spike's employer, had been marked down as a possible confederate.

It tickled him to think that both these giant brains

P.G. Wodehouse

should be so greatly exercised on his account.

He had been watching Molly closely during these days. So far, no announcement of the engagement had been made. It struck him that possibly it was being reserved for public mention on the night of the theatricals. The whole county would be at the castle then. There could be no more fitting moment. He sounded Lord Dreever, and the latter said moodily that he was probably right.

"There's going to be a dance of sorts after the show," he said, "and it'll be done then, I suppose. No getting out of it after that. It'll be all over the county. Trust my uncle for that. He'll get on a table, and shout it, shouldn't wonder. And it'll be in the Morning Post next day, and Katie'll see it! Only two days more, oh, lord!"

Jimmy deduced that Katie was the Savoy girl, concerning whom his lordship had vouchsafed no particulars save that she was a ripper and hadn't a penny.

Only two days! Like the battle of Waterloo, it was going to be a close-run affair. More than ever now, he realized how much Molly meant to him; and there were moments when it seemed to him that she, too, had begun to understand. That night on the terrace seemed somehow to have changed their relationship. He thought he had got closer to her. They were in touch. Before, she had been frank, cheerful, unembarrassed. Now, he noticed a constraint in her manner, a curious shyness. There was a barrier between them, but it was not the old barrier. He had ceased to be one of a crowd.

But it was a race against time. The first day slipped by,

a blank, and the second; till, now, it was but a matter of hours. The last afternoon had come.

Not even Mr. Samuel Galer, of Dodson's Private Inquiry Agency, could have kept a more unflagging watch than did Jimmy during those hours. There was no rehearsal that afternoon, and the members of the company, in various stages of nervous collapse, strayed distractedly about the grounds. First one, then another, would seize upon Molly, while Jimmy, watching from afar, cursed their pertinacity.

At last, she wondered off alone, and Jimmy, quitting his ambush, followed.

She walked in the direction of the lake. It had been a terribly hot, oppressive afternoon. There was thunder in the air. Through the trees, the lake glittered invitingly.

She was standing at the water's edge when Jimmy came up. Her back was turned. She was rocking with her foot a Canadian canoe that lay alongside the bank. She started as he spoke. His feet on the soft turf had made no sound.

"Can I take you out on the lake?" he said.

She did not answer for a moment. She was plainly confused.

"I'm sorry," she said. "I - I'm waiting for lord Dreever."

Jimmy saw that she was nervous. There was tension in the air. She was looking away from him, out across the lake, and her face was flushed.

"Won't you?" he said.

"I'm sorry," she said again.

Jimmy looked over his shoulder. Down the lower terrace was approaching the long form of his lordship. He walked with pensive jerkiness, not as one hurrying to a welcome tryst. As Jimmy looked, he vanished behind the great clump of laurels that stood on the lowest terrace. In another minute, he would reappear round them.

Gently, but with extreme dispatch, Jimmy placed a hand on either side of Molly's waist. The next moment, he had swung her off her feet, and lowered her carefully to the cushions in the bow of the canoe.

Then, jumping in himself with a force that made the boat rock, he loosened the mooring-rope, seized the paddle, and pushed off.

CHAPTER XIX

ON THE LAKE

In making love, as in every other branch of life, consistency is the quality most to be aimed at. To hedge is fatal. A man must choose the line of action that he judges to be best suited to his temperament, and hold to it without deviation. If Lochinvar snatches the maiden up on his saddle-bow, he must continue in that vein. He must not fancy that, having accomplished the feat, he can resume the episode on lines of devotional humility. Prehistoric man, who conducted his courtship with a club, never fell into the error of apologizing when his bride complained of headache.

Jimmy did not apologize. The idea did not enter his mind. He was feeling prehistoric. His heart was beating fast, and his mind was in a whirl, but the one definite thought that came to him during the first few seconds of the journey was that he ought to have done this earlier. This was the right way. Pick her up and carry her off, and leave uncles and fathers and butter-haired peers of the realm to look after themselves. This was the way. Alone together in their own little world of water, with nobody to interrupt and nobody to overhear! He should have done it before. He had wasted precious, golden time, hanging about while futile men chattered to her of things that could not

P.G. Wodehouse

possibly be of interest. But he had done the right thing at last. He had got her. She must listen to him now. She could not help listening. They were the only inhabitants of this new world.

He looked back over his shoulder at the world they had left. The last of the Dreevers had rounded the clump of laurels, and was standing at the edge of the water, gazing perplexedly after the retreating canoe.

"These poets put a thing very neatly sometimes," said Jimmy reflectively, as he dug the paddle into the water. "The man who said, 'Distance lends enchantment to the view,' for instance. Dreever looks quite nice when you see him as far away as this, with a good strip of water in between."

Molly, gazing over the side of the boat into the lake, abstained from feasting her eyes on the picturesque spectacle.

"Why did you do it?" she said, in a low voice.

Jimmy shipped the paddle, and allowed the canoe to drift. The ripple of the water against the prow sounded clear and thin in the stillness. The world seemed asleep. The sun blazed down, turning the water to flame. The air was hot, with the damp electrical heat that heralds a thunderstorm. Molly's face looked small and cool in the shade of her big hat. Jimmy, as he watched her, felt that he had done well. This was, indeed, the way.

"Why did you do it?" she said again.

"I had to."

"Take me back."

"No."

He took up the paddle, and placed a broader strip of water between the two worlds; then paused once more.

"I have something to say to you first," he said.

She did not answer. He looked over his shoulder again. His lordship had disappeared.

"Do you mind if I smoke?"

She nodded. He filled his pipe carefully, and lighted it. The smoke moved sluggishly up through the still air. There was a long silence. A fish jumped close by, falling back in a shower of silver drops. Molly started at the sound, and half-turned.

"That was a fish," she said, as a child might have done.

Jimmy knocked the ashes out of his pipe.

"What made you do it?" he asked abruptly, echoing her own question.

She drew her fingers slowly through the water without speaking.

"You know what I mean. Dreever told me."

She looked up with a flash of spirit, which died away as she spoke.

"What right?" She stopped, and looked away again.

"None," said Jimmy. "But I wish you would tell me."

She hung her head. Jimmy bent forward, and touched her hand.

"Don't" he said; "for God's sake, don't! You mustn't."

"I must," she said, miserably.

"You sha'n't. It's wicked."

"I must. It's no good talking about it. It's too late."

"It's not. You must break it off to-day."

She shook her head. Her fingers still dabbled mechanically in the water. The sun was hidden now behind a gray veil, which deepened into a sullen black over the hill behind the castle. The heat had grown more oppressive, with a threat of coming storm.

"What made you do it?" he asked again.

"Don't let's talk about it ... Please!"

He had a momentary glimpse of her face. There were tears in her eyes. At the sight, his self-control snapped.

"You sha'n't," he cried. "It's ghastly. I won't let you. You must understand now. You must know what you are to me. Do you think I shall let you - ?"

A low growl of thunder rumbled through the stillness, like the muttering of a sleepy giant. The black cloud that had hung over the hill had crept closer. The heat was stifling. In the middle of the lake, some fifty yards distant, lay the island, cool and mysterious in the gathering darkness.

Jimmy broke off, and seized the paddle.

On this side of the island was a boathouse, a little creek covered over with boards and capable of sheltering an ordinary rowboat. He ran the canoe in just as the storm began, and turned her broadside on, so that they could watch the rain, which was sweeping over the lake in sheets.

He began to speak again, more slowly now.

"I think I loved you from the first day I saw you on the ship. And, then, I lost you. I found you again by a miracle, and lost you again. I found you here by another miracle, but this time I am not going to lose you. Do you think I'm going to stand by and see you taken from me by - by - "

He took her hand.

"Molly, you can't love him. It isn't possible. If I thought you did, I wouldn't try to spoil your happiness. I'd go away. But you don't. You can't. He's nothing. Molly!"

The canoe rocked as he leaned toward her.

"Molly!"

She said nothing; but, for the first time, her eyes met his, clear and unwavering. He could read fear in them, fear - not of himself, of something vague, something he could not guess at. But they shone with a light that

P.G. Wodehouse

conquered the fear as the sun conquers fire; and he drew her to him, and kissed her again and again, murmuring incoherently.

Suddenly, she wrenched herself away, struggling like some wild thing. The boat plunged.

"I can't," she cried in a choking voice. "I mustn't. Oh, I can't!"

He stretched out a hand, and clutched at the rail than ran along the wall. The plunging ceased. He turned. She had hidden her face, and was sobbing, quietly, with the forlorn hopelessness of a lost child.

He made a movement toward her, but drew back. He felt dazed.

The rain thudded and splashed on the wooden roof. A few drops trickled through a crack in the boards. He took off his coat, and placed it gently over her shoulders.

"Molly!"

She looked up with wet eyes.

"Molly, dear, what is it?"

"I mustn't. It isn't right."

"I don't understand."

"I mustn't, Jimmy."

He moved cautiously forward, holding the rail, till he

was at her side, and took her in his arms.

"What is it, dear? Tell me."

She clung to him without speaking.

"You aren't worrying about him, are you - about Dreever? There's nothing to worry about. It'll be quite easy and simple. I'll tell him, if you like. He knows you don't care for him; and, besides, there's a girl in London that he - "

"No, no. It's not that."

"What is it, dear? What's troubling you?"

"Jimmy - " She stopped.

He waited.

"Yes?"

"Jimmy, my father wouldn't - father - father - does-n't - "

"Doesn't like me?"

She nodded miserably.

A great wave of relief swept over Jimmy. He had imagined - he hardly knew what he had imagined: some vast, insuperable obstacle; some tremendous catastrophe, whirling them asunder. He could have laughed aloud in his happiness. So, this was it, this was the cloud that brooded over them - that Mr. McEachern did not like him! The angel, guarding Eden with a fiery sword, had changed into a policeman with a truncheon.

"He must learn to love me," he said, lightly.

She looked at him hopelessly. He could not see; he could not understand. And how could she tell him? Her father's words rang in her brain. He was "crooked." He was "here on some game." He was being watched. But she loved him, she loved him! Oh, how could she make him understand?

She clung tighter to him, trembling. He became serious again. "Dear, you mustn't worry," he said. "It can't be helped. He'll come round. Once we're married - "

"No, no. Oh, can't you understand? I couldn't, I couldn't!"

Jimmy's face whitened. He looked at her anxiously.

"But, dear!" he said. "You can't - do you mean to say - will that - " he searched for a word-"stop you?" he concluded.

"It must," she whispered.

A cold hand clutched at his heart. His world was falling to pieces, crumbling under his eyes.

"But - but you love me," he said, slowly. It was as if he were trying to find the key to a puzzle. "I - don't see."

"You couldn't. You can't. You're a man. You don't know. It's so different for a man! He's brought up all his life with the idea of leaving home. He goes away naturally."

"But, dear, you couldn't live at home all your life. Whoever you married - "

"But this would be different. Father would never speak to me again. I should never see him again. He would go right out of my life. Jimmy, I couldn't. A girl can't cut away twenty years of her life, and start fresh like that. I should be haunted. I should make you miserable. Every day, a hundred little things would remind me of him, and I shouldn't be strong enough to resist them. You don't know how fond he is of me, how good he has always been. Ever since I can remember, we've been such friends. You've only seen the outside of him, and I know how different that is from what he really is. All his life he has thought only of me. He has told me things about himself which nobody else dreams of, and I know that all these years he has been working just for me. Jimmy, you don't hate me for saying this, do you?"

"Go on," he said, drawing her closer to him.

"I can't remember my mother. She died when I was quite little. So, he and I have been the only ones - till you came."

Memories of those early days crowded her mind as she spoke, making her voice tremble; half-forgotten trifles, many of them, fraught with the glamour and fragrance of past happiness.

"We have always been together. He trusted me, and I trusted him, and we saw things through together. When I was ill, he used to sit up all night with me, night after night. Once - I'd only got a little fever, really, but I thought I was terribly bad - I heard him come in late, and called out to him, and he came straight in, and sat and held my hand all through the night; and it was only by accident I found out later that it had been raining and that he was soaked through. It might have killed him. We were partners, Jimmy, dear. I couldn't do anything to hurt him now, could I? It wouldn't be square."

Jimmy had turned away his head, for fear his face might betray what he was feeling. He was in a hell of unreasoning jealousy. He wanted her, body and soul, and every word she said bit like a raw wound. A moment before, and he had felt that she belonged to him. Now, in the first shock of reaction, he saw himself a stranger, an intruder, a trespasser on holy ground.

She saw the movement, and her intuition put her in touch with his thoughts.

"No, no," she cried; "no, Jimmy, not that!"

Their eyes met, and he was satisfied.

They sat there, silent. The rain had lessened its force, and was falling now in a gentle shower. A strip of blue sky, pale and watery, showed through the gray over the hills. On the island close behind them, a thrush had begun to sing.

"What are we to do?" she said, at last. "What can we do?"

"We must wait," he said. "It will all come right. It must. Nothing can stop us now."

The rain had ceased. The blue had routed the gray, and

driven it from the sky. The sun, low down in the west, shone out bravely over the lake. The air was cool and fresh.

Jimmy's spirits rose with a bound. He accepted the omen. This was the world as it really was, smiling and friendly, not gray, as he had fancied it. He had won. Nothing could alter that. What remained to be done was trivial. He wondered how he could ever have allowed it to weigh upon him.

After awhile, he pushed the boat out of its shelter on to the glittering water, and seized the paddle.

"We must be getting back," he said. "I wonder what the time is. I wish we could stay out forever. But it must be late. Molly!"

"Yes?"

"Whatever happens, you'll break off this engagement with Dreever? Shall I tell him? I will if you like."

"No, I will. I'll write him a note, if I don't see him before dinner."

Jimmy paddled on a few strokes.

"It's no good," he said suddenly, "I can't keep it in. Molly, do you mind if I sing a bar or two? I've got a beastly voice, but I'm feeling rather happy. I'll stop as soon as I can."

He raised his voice discordantly.

Covertly, from beneath the shade of her big hat, Molly

watched him with troubled eyes. The sun had gone down behind the hills, and the water had ceased to glitter. There was a suggestion of chill in the air. The great mass of the castle frowned down upon them, dark and forbidding in the dim light.

She shivered.

CHAPTER XX

A LESSON IN PICQTUET

Lord Dreever, meanwhile, having left the waterside, lighted a cigarette, and proceeded to make a reflective tour of the grounds. He felt aggrieved with the world. Molly's desertion in the canoe with Jimmy did not trouble him: he had other sorrows. One is never at one's best and sunniest when one has been forced by a ruthless uncle into abandoning the girl one loves and becoming engaged to another, to whom one is indifferent. Something of a jaundiced tinge stains one's outlook on life in such circumstances. Moreover, Lord Dreever was not by nature an introspective young man, but, examining his position as he walked along, he found himself wondering whether it was not a little unheroic. He came to the conclusion that perhaps it was. Of course, Uncle Thomas could make it deucedly unpleasant for him if he kicked. That was the trouble. If only he had even - say, a couple of thousands a year of his own - he might make a fight for it. But, dash it, Uncle Tom could cut off supplies to such a frightful extent, if there was trouble, that he would have to go on living at Dreever indefinitely, without so much as a fearful quid to call his own.

Imagination boggled at the prospect. In the summer and autumn, when there was shooting, his lordship was not indisposed to a stay at the home of his fathers. But all the year round! Better a broken heart inside the radius than a sound one in the country in the winter.

"But, by gad!" mused his lordship; "if I had as much as a couple - yes, dash it, even a couple of thousand a year, I'd chance it, and ask Katie to marry me, dashed if I wouldn't!"

He walked on, drawing thoughtfully at his cigarette. The more he reviewed the situation, the less he liked it. There was only one bright spot in it, and this was the feeling that now money must surely get a shade less tight. Extracting the precious ore from Sir Thomas hitherto had been like pulling back-teeth out of a bull-dog. But, now, on the strength of this infernal engagement, surely the uncle might reasonably be expected to scatter largesse to some extent.

His lordship was just wondering whether, if approached in a softened mood, the other might not disgorge something quite big, when a large, warm rain-drop fell on his hand. From the bushes round about came an ever increasing patter. The sky was leaden.

He looked round him for shelter. He had reached the rose-garden in the course of his perambulations. At the far end was a summerhouse. He turned up his coat-collar, and ran.

As he drew near, he heard a slow and dirge-like whistling proceeding from the interior. Plunging in out of breath, just as the deluge began, he found Hargate seated at the little wooden table with an earnest expression on his face. The table was covered with cards. Hargate had not yet been compelled to sprain his wrist, having adopted the alternative of merely refusing invitations to play billiards.

"Hello, Hargate," said his lordship. "Isn't it coming down, by Jove!"

Hargate glanced up, nodded without speaking, and turned his attention to the cards once more. He took one from the pack in his left hand, looked at it, hesitated for a moment, as if doubtful whereabouts on the table it would produce the most artistic effect; and finally put it face upward. Then, he moved another card from the table, and put it on top of the other one. Throughout the performance, he whistled painfully.

His lordship regarded his guest with annoyance.

"That looks frightfully exciting," he said, disparagingly. "What are you playing at? Patience?"

Hargate nodded again, this time without looking up.

"Oh, don't sit there looking like a frog," said Lord Dreever, irritably. "Talk, man."

Hargate gathered up the cards, and proceeded to shuffle them in a meditative manner, whistling the while.

"Oh, stop it!" said his lordship.

Hargate nodded, and obediently put down the deck.

"Look here." said Lord Dreever, "this is boring me stiff. Let's have a game of something. Anything to pass away the time. Curse this rain! We shall be cooped up here till dinner at this rate. Ever played picquet? I could teach it you in five minutes."

A look almost of awe came into Hargate's face, the look of one who sees a miracle performed before his eyes. For years, he had been using all the large stock of diplomacy at his command to induce callow youths to play picquet with him, and here was this – admirable young man, this pearl among young men, positively offering to teach him the game. It was too much happiness. What had he done to deserve this? He felt as a toil-worn lion might feel if some antelope, instead of making its customary bee-line for the horizon, were to trot up and insert its head between his jaws.

"I - I shouldn't mind being shown the idea," he said.

He listened attentively while Lord Dreever explained at some length the principles that govern the game of picquet. Every now and then, he asked a question. It was evident that he was beginning to grasp the idea of the game.

"What exactly is re-piquing?" he asked, as his, lordship paused.

"It's like this," said his lordship, returning to his lecture.

"Yes, I see now," said the neophyte.

They began playing. Lord Dreever, as was only to be expected in a contest between teacher and student, won the first two hands. Hargate won the next.

"I've got the hang of it all right now," he said,

complacently. "It's a simple sort of game. Make it more exciting, don't you think, if we played for something?"

"All right," said Lord Dreever slowly, "if you like."

He would not have suggested it himself, but, after all, dash it, if the man really asked for it - It was not his fault if the winning of a hand should have given the fellow the impression that he knew all there was to be known about picquet. Of course, picquet was a game where skill was practically bound to win. But - after all, Hargate probably had plenty of money. He could afford it.

"All right," said his lordship again. "How much?"

"Something fairly moderate? Ten bob a hundred?"

There is no doubt that his lordship ought at this suggestion to have corrected the novice's notion that ten shillings a hundred was fairly moderate. He knew that it was possible for a poor player to lose four hundred points in a twenty minutes' game, and usual for him to lose two hundred. But he let the thing go.

"Very well," he said.

Twenty minutes later, Hargate was looking some-what ruefully at the score-sheet. "I owe you eighteen shillings," he said. "Shall I pay you now, or shall we settle up in a lump after we've finished?"

"What about stopping now?" said Lord Dreever. "It's quite fine out."

"No, let's go on. I've nothing to do till dinner, and I don't suppose you have."

His lordship's conscience made one last effort.

"You'd much better stop, you know, Hargate, really," he said. "You can lose a frightful lot at this game."

"My dear Dreever," said Hargate stiffly, "I can look after myself, thanks. Of course, if you think you are risking too much, by all means - "

"Oh, if you don't mind," said his lordship, outraged, "I'm only too frightfully pleased. Only, remember I warned you."

"I'll bear it in mind. By the way, before we start, care to make it a sovereign a hundred?"

Lord Dreever could not afford to play picquet for a soverign a hundred, or, indeed, to play picquet for money at all; but, after his adversary's innuendo, it was impossible for a young gentleman of spirit to admit the humiliating fact. He nodded.

"About time, I fancy," said Hargate, looking at his watch an hour later, "that we were going in to dress for dinner."

His lordship, made no reply. He was wrapped in thought.

"Let's see, that's twenty pounds you owe me, isn't it?" continued Hargate. "Shocking bad luck you had!"

They went out into the rose-garden.

"Jolly everything smells after the rain," said Hargate, who seemed to have struck a conversational patch. "Freshened everything up."

His lordship did not appear to have noticed it. He seemed to be thinking of something else. His air was pensive and abstracted.

"There's just time," said Hargate, looking at his watch again, "for a short stroll. I want to have a talk with you."

"Oh!" said Lord Dreever.

His air did not belie his feelings. He looked pensive, and was pensive. It was deuced awkward, this twenty pounds business.

Hargate was watching him covertly. It was his business to know other people's business, and he knew that Lord Dreever was impecunious, and depended for supplies entirely on a prehensile uncle. For the success of the proposal he was about to make, he depended on this fact.

"Who's this man Pitt?" asked Hargate.

"Oh, pal of mine," said his lordship. "Why?"

"I can't stand the fellow."

"I think he's a good chap," said his lordship. "In fact," remembering Jimmy's Good Samaritanism, "I know he is. Why don't you like him?"

"I don't know. I don't."

"Oh?" said his lordship, indifferently. He was in no mood to listen to the likes and dislikes of other men.

"Look here, Dreever," said Hargate, "I want you to do something for me. I want you to get Pitt out of the place."

Lord Dreever eyed his guest curiously.

"Eh?" he said.

Hargate repeated his remark.

"You seem to have mapped out quite a program for me," said Lord Dreever.

"Get him out of it," continued Hargate vehemently. Jimmy's prohibition against billiards had hit him hard. He was suffering the torments of Tantalus. The castle was full of young men of the kind to whom he most resorted, easy marks every one; and here he was, simply through Jimmy, careened like a disabled battleship. It was maddening. "Make him go. You invited him here. He doesn't expect to stop indefinitely, I suppose? If you left, he'd have to, too. What you must do is to go back to London to-morrow. You can easily make some excuse. He'll have to go with you. Then, you can drop him in London, and come back. That's what you must do."

A delicate pink flush might have been seen to spread itself over Lord Dreever's face. He began to look like an angry rabbit. He had not a great deal of pride in his composition, but the thought of the ignominious role that Hargate was sketching out for him stirred what he had to its shallow bottom. Talking on, Hargate managed to add the last straw.

"Of course," he said, "that money you lost to me at picquet - what was it? Twenty? Twenty pounds, wasn't it? Well, we would look on that as canceled, of course. That will be all right."

His lordship exploded.

"Will it?" he cried, pink to the ears. "Will it, by George? I'll pay you every frightful penny of it to-morrow, and then you can clear out, instead of Pitt. What do you take me for, I should like to know?"

"A fool, if you refuse my offer."

"I've a jolly good mind to give you a most frightful kicking."

"I shouldn't try, if I were you. It's not the sort of game you'd shine at. Better stick to picquet."

"If you think I can't pay your rotten money - "

"I do. But, if you can, so much the better. Money is always useful."

"I may be a fool in some ways - "

"You understate it, my dear man."

" - but I'm not a cad."

"You're getting quite rosy, Dreever. Wrath is good for the complexion."

"And, if you think you can bribe me, you never made a bigger mistake in your life."

"Yes, I did," said Hargate, "when I thought you had some glimmerings of intelligence. But, if it gives you any pleasure to behave like the juvenile lead in a melodrama, by all means do. Personally, I shouldn't have thought the game would be worth the candle. But, if your keen sense of honor compels you to pay the twenty pounds, all right. You mentioned to-morrow? That will suit me. So, we'll let it go it at that."

He walked off, leaving Lord Dreever filled with the comfortable glow that comes to the weak man who for once has displayed determination. He felt that he must not go back from his dignified standpoint. That money would have to be paid, and on the morrow. Hargate was the sort of man who could, and would, make it exceedingly unpleasant for him if he failed. A debt of honor was not a thing to be trifled with.

But he felt quite safe. He knew he could get the money when he pleased. It showed, he reflected philosophically, how out of evil cometh good. His greater misfortune, the engagement, would, as it were, neutralize the less, for it was ridiculous to suppose that Sir Thomas, having seen his ends accomplished, and being presumably in a spacious mood in consequence, would not be amenable to a request for a mere twenty pounds.

He went on into the hall. He felt strong and capable. He had shown Hargate the stuff there was in him. He was Spennie Dreever, the man of blood and iron, the man with whom it were best not to trifle. But it was really, come to think of it, uncommonly lucky that he was engaged to Molly. He recoiled from the idea of attempting, unfortified by that fact, to extract twenty pounds from Sir Thomas for a card-debt.

In the hall, he met Saunders.

"I have been looking for your lordship," said the butler.

"Eh? Well, here I am."

"Just so, your lordship. Miss McEachern entrusted me with this note to deliver to you in the event of her not being h'able to see you before dinner personally, your lordship."

"Right ho. Thanks."

He started to go upstairs, opening the envelope as he went. What could the girl be writing to him about? Surely, she wasn't going to start sending him love-letters, or any of that frightful rot? Deuced difficult it would be to play up to that sort of thing!

He stopped on the first landing to read the note, and at the opening line his jaw fell. The envelope fluttered to the ground.

"Oh, my sainted aunt!" he moaned, clutching at the banisters. "Now, I am in the soup!"

CHAPTER XXI

LOATHSOME GIFTS

There are doubtless men so constructed that they can find themselves accepted suitors without any particular whirl of emotion. King Solomon probably belonged to this class, and even Henry the Eighth must have become a trifle blase in time. But, to the average man, the sensations are complex and overwhelming. A certain stunned feeling is perhaps predominant. Blended with this is relief, the relief of a general who has brought a difficult campaign to a successful end, or of a member of a forlorn hope who finds that the danger is over and that he is still alive. To this must be added a newly born sense of magnificence. Our suspicion that we were something rather out of the ordinary run of men is suddenly confirmed. Our bosom heaves with complacency, and the world has nothing more to offer.

With some, there is an alloy of apprehension in the metal of their happiness, and the strain of an engagement sometimes brings with it even a faint shadow of regret. "She makes me buy things," one swain, in the third quarter of his engagement, was overheard to moan to a friend. "Two new ties only yesterday." He seemed to be debating with himself whether human nature could stand the strain.

But, whatever tragedies may cloud the end of the period, its beginning at least is bathed in sunshine.

Jimmy, regarding his lathered face in. the glass as he dressed for dinner that night, marveled at the excellence of t his best of allpossible worlds.

No doubts disturbed him. That the relations between Mr. McEachern and himself offered a permanent bar to his prospects, he did not believe. For the moment, he declined to consider the existence of the ex-constable at all. In a world that contained Molly, there was no room for other people. They were not in the picture. They did not exist.

To him, musing contentedly over the goodness of life, there entered, in the furtive manner habitual to that unreclaimed buccaneer, Spike Mullins. It may have been that Jimmy read his own satisfaction and happiness into the faces of others, but it certainly seemed to him that there was a sort of restrained joyousness about Spike's demeanor. The Bowery boy's shuffles on the carpet were almost a dance. His face seemed to glow beneath his crimson hair.

"Well," said Jimmy, "and how goes the world with young Lord Fitz-Mullins? Spike, have you ever been best man?

"What's dat, boss?"

"Best man at a wedding. Chap who stands by the bridegroom with a hand on the scruff of his neck to see that he goes through with it. Fellow who looks after everything, crowds the money on to the minister at the end of the ceremony, and then goes off and mayries the first bridesmaid, and lives happily ever."

Spike shook his head.

"I ain't got no use for gittin' married, boss."

"Spike, the misogynist! You wait, Spike. Some day, love will awake in your heart, and you'll start writing poetry."

"I'se not dat kind of mug, boss," protested the Bowery boy. "I ain't got no use fer goils. It's a mutt's game."

This was rank heresy. Jimmy laid down the razor from motives of prudence, and proceeded to lighten Spike's reprehensible darkness.

"Spike, you're an ass," he said. "You don't know anything about it. If you had any sense at all, you'd understand that the only thing worth doing in life is to get married. You bone-headed bachelors make me sick. Think what it would mean to you, having a wife. Think of going out on a cold winter's night to crack a crib, knowing that there would be a cup of hot soup waiting for you when you got back, and your slippers all warmed and comfortable. And then she'd sit on your knee, and you'd tell her how you shot the policeman, and you'd examine the swag together - ! Why, I can't imagine anything cozier. Perhaps there would be little Spikes running about the house. Can't you see them jumping with joy as you slid in through the window, and told the great news? 'Fahzer's killed a pleeceman!' cry the tiny, eager voices. Candy is served out all round in honor of the event. Golden-haired little Jimmy Mullins, my god-son, gets a dime for having thrown a stone at a plain-clothes detective that afternoon. All is joy and wholesome revelry. Take my word for it, Spike, there's nothing like domesticity."

"Dere was a goil once," said Spike, meditatively. "Only, I was never her steady. She married a cop."

"She wasn't worthy of you, Spike," said Jimmy, sympathetically. "A girl capable of going to the bad like that would never have done for you. You must pick some nice, sympathetic girl with a romantic admiration for your line of business. Meanwhile, let me finish shaving, or I shall be late for dinner. Great doings on to-night, Spike."

Spike became animated.

"Sure, boss I Dat's just what - "

"If you could collect all the blue blood that will be under this roof to-night, Spike, into one vat, you'd be able to start a dyeing-works. Don't try, though. They mightn't like it. By the way, have you seen anything more - of course, you have. What I mean is, have you talked at all with that valet man, the one you think is a detective?"

"Why, boss, dat's just - "

"I hope for his own sake he's a better performer than my old friend, Galer. That man is getting on my nerves, Spike. He pursues me like a smell-dog. I expect he's lurking out in the passage now. Did you see him?"

"Did I! Boss! Why - "

Jimmy inspected Spike gravely.

"Spike," he said, "there's something on your mind. You're trying to say something. What is it? Out with it."

Spike's excitement vented itself in a rush of words.

"Gee, boss! There's bin doin's to-night fer fair, lie coco's still buzzin'. Sure t'ing! Why, say, when I was to Sir Tummas' dressin'-room dis afternoon - "

"What!"

"Surest t'ing you know. Just before de storm come on, when it was all as dark as could be. Well, I was - "

Jimmy interrupted.

"In Sir Thomas's dressing-room! What the - "

Spike looked somewhat embarrassed. He grinned apologetically, and shuffled his feet.

"I've got dem, boss!" he said, with a smirk.

"Got them? Got what?"

"Dese."

Spike plunged a hand in a pocket, and drew forth in a glittering mass Lady Julia Blunt's rope of diamonds.

CHAPTER XXII

TWO OF A TRADE DISAGREE

"One hundred t'ousand plunks," murmured Spike, gazing lovingly at them. "I says to myself, de boss ain't got no time to be gittin' after dem himself. He's too busy dese days wit' jollyin' along de swells. So, it's up to me, I says, 'cos de boss'll be tickled to deat', all right, all right, if we can git away wit' dem. So, I - "

Jimmy gave tongue with an energy that amazed his faithful follower. The nightmare horror of the situation had affected him much as a sudden blow in the parts about the waistcoat might have done. But, now, as Spike would have said, he caught up with his breath. The smirk faded slowly from the other's face as he listened. Not even in the Bowery, full as it was of candid friends, had he listened to such a trenchant summing-up of his mental and moral deficiencies.

"Boss!" he protested.

"That's just a sketchy outline," said Jimmy, pausing for breath. "I can't do you justice impromptu like this - you're too vast and overwhelming."

"But, boss, what's eatin' you? Ain't youse tickled?"

P.G. Wodehouse

"Tickled!" Jimmy sawed the air. "Tickled! You lunatic! Can't you see what you've done?"

"I've got dem," said Spike, whose mind was not readily receptive of new ideas. It seemed to him that Jimmy missed the main point.

"Didn't I tell you there was nothing doing when you wanted to take those things the other day?"

Spike's face cleared. As he had suspected, Jimmy had missed the point.

"Why, say, boss, yes. Sure! But dose was little, dinky t'ings. Of course, youse wouldn't stand fer swipin' chicken-feed like dem. But dese is different. Dese di'monds is boids. It's one hundred t'ousand plunks fer dese."

"Spike," said Jimmy with painful calm.

"Huh?"

"Will you listen for a moment?"

"Sure."

"I know it's practically hopeless. To get an idea into your head, one wants a proper outfit - drills, blasting-powder, and so on. But there's just a chance, perhaps, if I talk slowly. Has it occurred to you, Spike, my bonny, blue-eyed Spike, that every other man, more or less, in this stately home of England, is a detective who has probably received instructions to watch you like a lynx? Do you imagine that your blameless past is a sufficient safeguard? I suppose you think that these detectives will say to themselves, 'Now, whom shall we suspect? We must leave out Spike Mullins, of course, because he naturally wouldn't dream of doing such a thing. It can't be dear old Spike who's got the stuff.'"

"But, boss," interposed Spike brightly, "I ain't! Dat's right. I ain't got it. Youse has!"

Jimmy looked at the speaker with admiration. After all, there was a breezy delirium about Spike's methods of thought that was rather stimulating when you got used to it. The worst of it was that it did not fit in with practical, everyday life. Under different conditions - say, during convivial evenings at Bloomingdale - he could imagine the Bowery boy being a charming companion. How pleasantly, for instance, such remarks as that last would while away the monotony of a padded cell!

"But, laddie," he said with steely affection, "listen once more. Reflect! Ponder! Does it not seep into your consciousness that we are, as it were, subtly connected in this house in the minds of certain bad persons? Are we not imagined by Mr. McEachern, for instance, to be working hand-in-hand like brothers? Do you fancy that Mr. McEachern, chatting with his tame sleuth-hound over their cigars, will have been reticent on this point? I think not. How do you propose to baffle that gentlemanly sleuth, Spike, who, I may mention once again, has rarely moved more than two yards away from me since his arrival?"

An involuntary chuckle escaped Spike.

"Sure, boss, dat's all right."

"All right, is it? Well, well! What makes you think it is all right?"

"Why, say, boss, dose sleut's is out of business." A merry grin split Spike's face. "It's funny, boss. Gee! It's got a circus skinned! Listen. Dey's bin an' arrest each other."

Jimmy moodily revised his former view. Even in Bloomingdale, this sort of thing would be coldly received. Genius must ever walk alone. Spike would have to get along without hope of meeting a kindred spirit, another fellow-being in tune with his brain-processes.

"Dat's right," chuckled Spike. "Leastways, it ain't."

"No, no," said Jimmy, soothingly. " I quite understand."

"It's dis way, boss. One of dem has bin an' arrest de odder mug. Dey had a scrap, each t'inkin' de odder guy was after de jools, an' not knowin' dey was bot' sleut's, an' now one of dem's bin an' taken de odder off, an'" - there were tears of innocent joy in Spike's eyes - "an' locked him into de coal-cellar."

"What on earth do you mean?"

Spike giggled helplessly.

"Listen, boss. It's dis way. Gee! It beat de band! When it's all dark 'cos of de storm comin' on, I'm in de dressin'-room, chasin' around fer de jool-box, an' just as I gits a line on it, gee! I hears a footstep comin' down de passage, very soft, straight fer de door. Was I to de bad? Dat's right. I says to meself, here's one of de sleut' guys what's bin and got wise to me, an' he's comin' in to put de grip on me. So, I gits up quick, an' I hides behind a coitain. Dere's a coitain at de side of de room. Dere's dude suits an' t'ings hangin' behind it. I chases meself in dere, and stands waitin' fer de sleut' to come in. 'Cos den, you see, I'm goin' to try an' get busy before he can see who I am - it's pretty dark 'cos of de storm - an' jolt him one on de point of de jaw, an' den, while he's down an' out, chase meself fer de soivants' hall."

"Yes?" said Jimmy.

"Well, dis guy, he gits to de door, an' opens it, an' I'm just gittin' ready fer one sudden boist of speed, when dere jumps out from de room on de odder side de passage - you know de room – anodder guy, an' gits de rapid strangleholt on de foist mug. Say, wouldn't dat make youse glad you hadn't gone to de circus? Honest, it was better dan Coney Island."

"Go on. What happened then?"

"Dey falls to scrappin' good an' hard. Dey couldn't see me, an' I couldn't see dem, but I could hear dem bumpin' about and sluggin' each other to beat de band. An', by and by, one of de mugs puts do odder mug to de bad, so dat he goes down and takes de count; an' den I hears a click. An' I know what dat is. It's one of de gazebos has put de irons on de odder gazebo."

"Call them A, and B.," suggested Jimmy.

"Den I hears him - de foist mug - strike a light, 'cos it's dark dere 'cos of de storm, an' den he says, 'Got youse.

have I?' he says. 'I've had my eye on youse, t'inkin' youse was up to somet'in' of dis kind. I've bin watching youse!' I knew de voice. It's dat mug what calls himself Sir Tummas' vally. An' de odder - "

Jimmy burst into a roar of laughter.

"Don't, Spike! This is more than man was meant to stand. Do you mean to tell me it is my bright, brainy, persevering friend Galer who has been handcuffed and locked in the coal-cellar?"

Spike grinned broadly.

"Sure, dat's right," he said.

"It's a judgment," said Jimmy, delightedly. "That's what it is! No man has a right to be such a consumate ass as Galer. It isn't decent."

There had been moments when McEachern's faithful employee had filled Jimmy with an odd sort of fury, a kind of hurt pride, almost to the extent of making him wish that he really could have been the desperado McEachern fancied him. Never in his life before had he sat still under a challenge, and this espionage had been one. Behind the clumsy watcher, he had seen always the self-satisfied figure of McEachern. If there had been anything subtle about the man from Dodson's, he could have forgiven him; but there was not. Years of practise had left Spike with a sort of sixth sense as regarded representatives of the law. He could pierce the most cunning disguise. But, in the case of Galer, even Jimmy could detect the detective.

"Go on," he said.

Spike proceeded.

"Well, de odder mug, de one down an' out on de floor wit' de irons on - "

"Galer, in fact," said Jimmy. "Handsome, dashing Galer!"

"Sure. Well, he's too busy catchin' up wit' his breat' to shoot it back swift, but, after he's bin doin' de deep-breathin' strut for a while, he says, 'You mutt,' he says, 'youse is to de bad. You've made a break, you have. Dat's right. Surest t'ing you know.' He puts it different, but dat's what he means. 'I'm a sleut', he says. 'Take dese t'ings off!' - meanin' de irons. Does de odder mug, de vally gazebo, give him de glad eye? Not so's you could notice it. He gives him de merry ha-ha. He says dat dat's de woist tale dat's ever bin handed to him. 'Tell it to Sweeney!' he says. 'I knows youse. Youse woims yourself into de house as a guest, when youse is really after de loidy's jools.' At dese crool woids, de odder mug, Galer, gits hot under de collar. 'I'm a sure-'nough sleut',' he says. 'I blows into dis house at de special request of Mr. McEachern, de American gent.' De odder mug hands de lemon again. 'Tell it to de King of Denmark,' he says. 'Dis cop's de limit. Youse has enough gall fer ten strong men,' he says. 'Show me to Mr. McEachern,' says Galer. 'He'll - ' crouch, is dat it?"

"Vouch?" suggested Jimmy. "Meaning give the glad hand to."

"Dat's right. Vouch. I wondered what he meant at de time. 'He'll vouch for me,' he says. Dat puts him all right, he t'inks; but no, he's still in Dutch, 'cos de vally mug says, 'Nix on dat! I ain't goin' to chase around de house wit' youse, lookin' fer Mr. McEachern. It's youse fer de coal-cellar, me man, an' we'll see what youse has to say when I makes me report to Sir Tummas.' 'Well, dat's to de good,' says Galer. 'Tell Sir Tummas. I'll explain to him.' 'Not me!' says de vally. 'Sir Tummas has a hard evenin's woik before him, jollyin' along de swells what's comin' to see dis stoige-piece dey're actin'. I ain't goin' to worry him till he's good and ready. To de coal-cellar fer yours! G'wan!' an' off dey goes! An' I gits busy ag'in, swipes de jools, an' chases meself here."

Jimmy wiped his eyes.

"Have you ever heard of poetic justice, Spike?" he asked. "This is it. But, in this hour of mirth and good-will, we must not forget - "

Spike interrupted. Pleased by the enthusiastic reception of his narrative, he proceeded to point out the morals that were to be deduced there-from.

"So, youse see, boss," he said, "it's all to de merry. When dey rubbers for de jools, an' finds dem gone, dey'll t'ink dis Galer guy swiped dem. Dey won't t'ink of us."

Jimmy looked at the speaker gravely.

"Of course," said he. "What a reasoner you are, Spike! Galer was just opening the door from the outside, by your account, when the valet man sprang at him. Naturally, they'll think that he took the jewels. Especially, as they won't find them on him. A man who can open a locked safe through a closed door is just the sort of fellow who would be able to get rid of the swag neatly while rolling about the floor with the valet. His not having the jewels will make the case all the blacker against him. And what will make them still more certain that he is the thief is that he really is a detective. Spike, you ought to be in some sort of a home, you know."

The Bowery boy looked disturbed.

"I didn't t'ink of dat, boss," he admitted.

"Of course not. One can't think of everything. Now, if you will just hand me those diamonds, I will put them back where they belong."

"Put dem back, boss!"

"What else would you propose? I'd get you to do it, only I don't think putting things back is quite in your line."

Spike handed over the jewels. The boss was the boss, and what he said went. But his demeanor was tragic, telling eloquently of hopes blighted.

Jimmy took the necklace with something of a thrill. He was a connoisseur of jewels, and a fine gem affected him much as a fine picture affects the artistic. He ran the diamonds through his fingers, then scrutinized them again, more closely this time.

Spike watched him with a slight return of hope. It seemed to him that the boss was wavering. Perhaps, now that he had actually handled the jewels, he would find it impossible to give them up. To Spike, a diamond necklace of cunning workmanship was merely the equivalent of so many "plunks"; but he knew that there were men, otherwise sane, who valued a jewel for its own sake.

"It's a boid of a necklace, boss," he murmured, encouragingly.

"It is," said Jimmy; "in its way, I've never seen anything much better. Sir Thomas will be glad to have it back."

"Den, you're goin' to put it back, boss?"

"I am," said Jimmy. "I'll do it just before the theatricals. There should be a chance, then. There's one good thing. This afternoon's affair will have cleared the air of sleuth-hounds a little."

CHAPTER XXIII

FAMILY JARS

Hildebrand Spencer Poynt de Burgh John Hannasyde Coombe-Crombie, twelfth Earl of Dreever, was feeling like a toad under the harrow. He read the letter again, but a second perusal made it no better. Very briefly and clearly, Molly had broken off the engagement. She "thought it best." She was "afraid it could make neither of us happy." All very true, thought his lordship miserably. His sentiments to a T. At the proper time, he would have liked nothing better. But why seize for this declaration the precise moment when he was intending, on the strength of the engagement, to separate his uncle from twenty pounds? That was what rankled. That Molly could have no knowledge of his sad condition did not occur to him. He had a sort of feeling that she ought to have known by instinct. Nature, as has been pointed out, had equipped Hildebrand Spencer Poynt de Burgh with one of those cheap-substitute minds. What passed for brain in him was to genuine gray matter as just-as-good imitation coffee is to real Mocha. In moments of emotion and mental stress, consequently, his reasoning, like Spike's, was apt to be in a class of its own.

He read the letter for the third time, and a gentle perspiration began to form on his forehead. This was

P.G. Wodehouse

awful. The presumable jubilation of Katie, the penniless ripper of the Savoy, when he should present himself to her a free man, did not enter into the mental picture that was unfolding before him. She was too remote. Between him and her lay the fearsome figure of Sir Thomas, rampant, filling the entire horizon. Nor is this to be wondered at. There was probably a brief space during which Perseus, concentrating his gaze upon the monster, did not see Andromeda; and a knight of the Middle Ages, jousting in the Gentlemen's Singles for a smile from his lady, rarely allowed the thought of that smile to occupy his whole mind at the moment when his boiler-plated antagonist was descending upon him in the wake of a sharp spear.

So with Spennie Dreever. Bright eyes might shine for him when all was over, but in the meantime what seemed to him more important was that bulging eyes would glare.

If only this had happened later - even a day later! The reckless impulsiveness of the modern girl had undone him. How was he to pay Hargate the money? Hargate must be paid. That was certain. No other course was possible. Lord Dreever's was not one of those natures that fret restlessly under debt. During his early career at college, he had endeared himself to the local tradesmen by the magnitude of the liabilities he had contracted with them. It was not the being in debt that he minded. It was the consequences. Hargate, he felt instinctively, was of a revengeful nature. He had given Hargate twenty pounds' worth of snubbing, and the latter had presented the bills. If it were not paid, things would happen. Hargate and he were members of the same club, and a member of a club who loses money at Cards to a fellow member, and fails to settle up, does not make himself popular with the committee.

He must get the money. There was no avoiding that conclusion. But how?

Financially, his lordship was like a fallen country with a glorious history. There had been a time, during his first two years at college, when he had reveled in the luxury of a handsome allowance. This was the golden age, when Sir Thomas Blunt, being, so to speak, new to the job, and feeling that, having reached the best circles, he must live up to them, had scattered largesse lavishly. For two years after his marriage with Lady Julia, he had maintained this admirable standard, crushing his natural parsimony. He had regarded the money so spent as capital sunk in an investment. By the end of the second year, he had found his feet, and began to look about him for ways of retrenchment. His lordship's allowance was an obvious way. He had not to wait long for an excuse for annihilating it. There is a game called poker, at which a man without much control over his features may exceed the limits of the handsomest allowance. His lordship's face during a game of poker was like the surface of some quiet pond, ruffled by every breeze. The blank despair of his expression when he held bad cards made bluffing expensive. The honest joy that bubbled over in his eyes when his hand was good acted as an efficient danger-signal to his grateful opponents. Two weeks of poker had led to his writing to his uncle a distressed, but confident, request for more funds; and the avuncular foot had come down with a joyous bang. Taking his stand on the evils of gambling, Sir Thomas had changed the conditions of the money-market for his nephew with a thoroughness that effectually prevented the possibility of the youth's being again caught by the fascinations of poker. The allowance vanished absolutely; and in its place there came into being an arrangement. By this, his lordship as to have whatever money he wished, but he must ask for it, and state why it was needed. If the request were reasonable, the cash would be forthcoming; if preposterous, it would not. The flaw in the scheme, from his lordship's point of view, was the difference of opinion that can exist in the minds of two men as to what the words reasonable and preposterous may be taken to mean.

Twenty pounds, for instance, would, in the lexicon of Sir Thomas Blunt, be perfectly reasonable for the current expenses of a man engaged to Molly McEachern, but preposterous for one to whom she had declined to remain engaged. It is these subtle shades of meaning that make the English language so full of pitfalls for the foreigner.

So engrossed was his lordship in his meditations that a voice spoke at his elbow ere he became aware of Sir Thomas himself, standing by his side.

"Well, Spennie, my boy," said the knight. "Time to dress for dinner, I think. Eh? Eh?"

He was plainly in high good humor. The thought of the distinguished company he was to entertain that night had changed him temporarily, as with some wave of a fairy wand, into a thing of joviality and benevolence. One could almost hear the milk of human kindness gurgling and splashing within him. The irony of fate! Tonight, such was his mood, a dutiful nephew could have come and felt in his pockets and helped himself - if circumstances had been different. Oh, woman, woman, how you bar us from paradise!

His lordship gurgled a wordless reply, thrusting the fateful letter hastily into his pocket. He would break the news anon. Soon - not yet - later on - in fact, anon!

"Up in your part, my boy?" continued Sir Thomas. "You mustn't spoil the play by forgetting your lines. That wouldn't do!"

His eye was caught by the envelope that Spennie had dropped. A momentary lapse from the jovial and benevolent was the result. His fussy little soul abhorred small untidinesses.

"Dear me," he said, stooping, "I wish people would not drop paper about the house. I cannot endure a litter." He spoke as if somebody had been playing hare-and-hounds, and scattering the scent on the stairs. This sort of thing sometimes made him regret the old days. In Blunt's Stores, Rule Sixty-seven imposed a fine of half-a-crown on employees convicted of paper-dropping.

"I - " began his lordship.

"Why" - Sir Thomas straightened himself - "it's addressed to you."

"I was just going to pick it up. It's - er - there was a note in it."

Sir Thomas gazed at the envelope again. Joviality and benevolence resumed their thrones.

"And in a feminine handwriting," he chuckled. He eyed the limp peer almost roguishly. "I see, I see," he said. "Very charming, quite delightful! Girls must have their little romance! I suppose you two young people are exchanging love-letters all day. Delightful, quite delightful! Don't look as if you were ashamed of it, my boy! I like it. I think it's charming."

Undoubtedly, this was the opening. Beyond a question, his lordship should have said at this point:

"Uncle, I cannot tell a lie. I cannot even allow myself to see you laboring under a delusion which a word from me can remove. The contents of this note are not what you suppose. They run as follows--"

What he did say was:

"Uncle, can you let me have twenty pounds?"

Those were his amazing words. They slipped out. He could not stop them.

Sir Thomas was taken aback for an instant, but not seriously. He started, as might a man who, stroking a cat, receives a sudden, but trifling scratch.

"Twenty pounds, eh?" he said, reflectively.

Then, the milk of human kindness swept over displeasure like a tidal wave. This was a night for rich gifts to the deserving.

"Why, certainly, my boy, certainly. Do you want it at once?"

His lordship replied that he did, please; and he had seldom said anything more fervently.

"Well, well. We'll see what we can do. Come with me."

He led the way to his dressing-room. Like nearly all the rooms at the castle, it was large. One wall was completely hidden by the curtain behind which Spike had taken refuge that afternoon.

Sir Thomas went to the dressing-table, and unlocked a small drawer.

"Twenty, you said? Five, ten, fifteen - here you are, my boy."

Lord Dreever muttered his thanks. Sir Thomas accepted the guttural acknowledgment with a friendly pat on the shoulder.

"I like a little touch like that," he said.

His lordship looked startled.

"I wouldn't have touched you," he began, "if it hadn't been - "

"A little touch like that letter-writing," Sir Thomas went on. "It shows a warm heart. She is a warm-hearted girl, Spennie. A charming, warm-hearted girl! You're uncommonly lucky, my boy."

His lordship, crackling the four bank-notes, silently agreed with him.

"But, come, I must be dressing. Dear me, it is very late. We shall have to hurry. By the way, my boy, I shall take the opportunity of making a public announcement of the engagement tonight. It will be a capital occasion for it. I think, perhaps, at the conclusion of the theatricals, a little speech - something quite impromptu and informal, just asking them to wish you happiness, and so on. I like the idea. There is an old-world air about it that appeals to me. Yes."

He turned to the dressing-table, and removed his collar.

"Well, run along, my boy," he said. "You must not be late." His lordship tottered from the room.

He did quite an unprecedented amount of thinking as he hurried into his evening clothes; but the thought occurring most frequently was that, whatever happened, all was well in one way, at any rate. He had the twenty pounds. There would be something colossal in the shape of disturbances when his uncle learned the truth. It would be the biggest thing since the San Francisco earthquake. But what of it? He had the money.

He slipped it into his waistcoat-pocket. He would take it down with him, and pay Hargate directly after dinner.

He left the room. The flutter of a skirt caught his eye as he reached the landing. A girl was coming down the corridor on the other side. He waited at the head of the stairs to let her go down before him. As she came on to the landing, he saw that it was Molly.

For a moment, there was an awkward pause.

"Er - I got your note," said his lordship.

She looked at him, and then burst out laughing.

"You know, you don't mind the least little bit," she said; "not a scrap. Now, do you?"

"Well, you see - "

"Don't make excuses! Do you?"

"Well, it's like this, you see, I - "

He caught her eye. Next moment, they were laughing together.

"No, but look here, you know," said his lordship. "What I mean is, it isn't that I don't - I mean, look here, there's no reason why we shouldn't be the best of pals."

"Why, of course, there isn't."

"No, really, I say? That's ripping. Shake hands on it."

They clasped hands; and it was in this affecting attitude that Sir Thomas Blunt, bustling downstairs, discovered them.

"Aha!" he cried, archly. "Well, well, well! But don't mind me, don't mind me!"

Molly flushed uncomfortably; partly, because she disliked Sir Thomas even when he was not arch, and hated him when he was; partly, because she felt foolish; and, principally, because she was bewildered. She had not looked forward to meeting Sir Thomas that night. It was always unpleasant to meet him, but it would be more unpleasant than usual after she had upset the scheme for which he had worked so earnestly. She had wondered whether he would be cold and distant, or voluble and heated. In her pessimistic moments, she had anticipated a long and painful scene. That he should be behaving like this was not very much short of a miracle. She could not understand it.

A glance at Lord Dreever enlightened her. That miserable creature was wearing the air of a timid child about to pull a large cracker. He seemed to be bracing himself up for an explosion.

She pitied him sincerely. So, he had not told his uncle the news, yet! Of course, he had scarcely had time. Saunders must have given him the note as he was going up to dress.

There was, however, no use in prolonging the agony. Sir Thomas must be told, sooner or later. She was glad of the chance to tell him herself. She would be able to explain that it was all her doing.

"I'm afraid there's a mistake," she said.

"Eh?" said Sir Thomas.

"I've been thinking it over, and I came to the conclusion that we weren't - well, I broke off the engagement!"

Sir Thomas' always prominent eyes protruded still further. The color of his florid face deepened. Suddenly, he chuckled.

Molly looked at him, amazed. Sir Thomas was indeed behaving unexpectedly to-night.

"I see it," he wheezed. "You're having a joke with me! So this is what you were hatching as I came downstairs! Don't tell me! If you had really thrown him over, you wouldn't have been laughing together like that. It's no good, my dear. I might have been taken in, if I had not seen you, but I did."

"No, no," cried Molly. "You're wrong. You're quite wrong. When you saw us, we were just agreeing that we should be very good friends. That was all. I broke off the engagement before that. I - "

She was aware that his lordship had emitted a hollow croak, but she took it as his method of endorsing her statement, not as a warning.

"I wrote Lord Dreever a note this evening," she went on, "telling him that I couldn't possibly - "

She broke off in alarm. With the beginning of her last speech, Sir Thomas had begun to swell, until now he looked as if he were in imminent danger of bursting. His face was purple. To Molly's lively imagination, his eyes appeared to move slowly out of his head, like a snail's. From the back of his throat came strange noises.

"S-s-so - " he stammered.

He gulped, and tried again.

"So this," he said, "so this - ! So that was what was in that letter, eh?"

Lord Dreever, a limp bundle against the banisters, smiled weakly.

"Eh?" yelled Sir Thomas.

His lordship started convulsively.

"Er, yes," he said, "yes, yes! That was it, don't you know!"

Sir Thomas eyed his nephew with a baleful stare. Molly looked from one to the other in bewilderment.

There was a pause, during which Sir Thomas seemed partially to recover command of himself. Doubts as to the propriety of a family row in mid-stairs appeared to occur to him. He moved forward.

"Come with me," he said, with awful curtness.

His lordship followed, bonelessly. Molly watched them go, and wondered more than ever. There was something behind this. It was not merely the breaking-off of the engagement that had roused Sir Thomas. He was not a just man, but he was just enough to be able to see that the blame was not Lord Dreever's. There had been something more. She was puzzled.

In the hall, Saunders was standing, weapon in hand, about to beat the gong.

"Not yet," snapped Sir Thomas. "Wait!"

Dinner had been ordered especially early that night because of the theatricals. The necessity for strict punctuality had been straitly enjoined upon Saunders. At some inconvenience, he had ensured strict punctuality. And now - But we all have our cross to bear in this world. Saunders bowed with dignified resignation.

Sir Thomas led the way into his study.

"Be so good as to close the door," he said.

His lordship was so good.

Sir Thomas backed to the mantelpiece, and stood there in the attitude which for generations has been sacred to the elderly Briton, feet well apart, hands clasped beneath his coat-tails. His stare raked Lord Dreever like a searchlight.

"Now, sir!" he said.

His lordship wilted before the gaze.

"The fact is, uncle - "

"Never mind the facts. I know them! What I require is an explanation."

He spread his feet further apart. The years had rolled back, and he was plain Thomas Blunt again, of Blunt's Stores, dealing with an erring employee.

"You know what I mean," he went on. "I am not referring to the breaking-off of the engagement. What I insist upon learning is your reason for failing to inform me earlier of the contents of that letter."

His lordship said that somehow, don't you know, there didn't seem to be a chance, you know. He had several times been on the point - but - well, some-how - well, that's how it was.

"No chance?" cried Sir Thomas. "Indeed! Why did you require that money I gave you?"

"Oh, er - I wanted it for something."

"Very possibly. For what?"

"I - the fact is, I owed it to a fellow."

"Ha! How did you come to owe it?"

His lordship shuffled.

"You have been gambling," boomed Sit Thomas "Am I right?"

"No, no. I say, no, no. It wasn't gambling. It was a game of skill. We were playing picquet."

"Kindly refrain from quibbling. You lost this money at cards, then, as I supposed. Just so."

He widened the space between his feet. He intensified his glare. He might have been posing to an illustrator of "Pilgrim's Progress" for a picture of "Apollyon straddling right across the way."

"So," he said, "you deliberately concealed from me the contents of that letter in order that you might extract money from me under false pretenses? Don't speak!" His lordship had gurgled, "You did! Your behavior was that of a - of a - "

There was a very fair selection of evil-doers in all

branches of business from which to choose. He gave the preference to the race-track.

" - of a common welsher," he concluded. "But I won't put up with it. No, not for an instant! I insist upon your returning that money to me here and now. If you have not got it with you, go and fetch it."

His lordship's face betrayed the deepest consternation. He had been prepared for much, but not for this. That he would have to undergo what in his school-days he would have called "a jaw" was inevitable, and he had been ready to go through with it. It might hurt his feelings, possibly, but it would leave his purse intact. A ghastly development of this kind he had not foreseen.

"But, I say, uncle!" he bleated.

Sir Thomas silenced him with a grand gesture.

Ruefully, his lordship produced his little all. Sir Thomas took it with a snort, and went to the door.

Saunders was still brooding statuesquely over the gong.

"Sound it!" said Sir Thomas.

Saunders obeyed him, with the air of an unleashed hound.

"And now," said Sir Thomas, "go to my dressing-room, and place these notes in the small drawer of the table."

The butler's calm, expressionless, yet withal observant eye took in at a glance the signs of trouble. Neither the inflated air of Sir Thomas nor the punctured-balloon bearing of Lord Dreever escaped him.

"Something h'up," he said to his immortal soul, as he moved upstairs. "Been a fair old, rare old row, seems to me!"

He reserved his more polished periods for use in public. In conversation with his immortal soul, he was wont to unbend somewhat.

CHAPTER XXIV

THE TREASURE SEEKER

Gloom wrapped his lordship about, during dinner, as with a garment. He owed twenty pounds. His assets amounted to seven shillings and four-pence. He thought, and thought again. Quite an intellectual pallor began to appear on his normally pink cheeks. Saunders, silently sympathetic - he hated Sir Thomas as an interloper, and entertained for his lordship, under whose father also he had served, a sort of paternal fondness - was ever at his elbow with the magic bottle; and to Spennie, emptying and re-emptying his glass almost mechanically, wine, the healer, brought an idea. To obtain twenty pounds from any one person of his acquaintance was impossible. To divide the twenty by four, and persuade a generous quartette to contribute five pounds apiece was more feasible.

Hope began to stir within him again.

Immediately after dinner, he began to flit about the castle like a family specter of active habits. The first person he met was Charteris.

"Hullo, Spennie," said Charteris, "I wanted to see you. It is currently reported that you are in love. At dinner, you looked as if you had influenza. What's your trouble? For goodness' sake, bear up till the show's over. Don't go swooning on the stage, or anything. Do you know your lines?"

"The fact is," said his lordship eagerly, "it's this way. I happen to want - Can you lend me a fiver?"

"All I have in the world at this moment," said Charteris, "is eleven shillings and a postage-stamp. If the stamp would be of any use to you as a start - ? No? You know, it's from small beginnings like that that great fortunes are amassed. However - "

Two minutes later, Lord Dreever had resumed his hunt.

The path of the borrower is a thorny one, especially if, like Spennie, his reputation as a payer-back is not of the best.

Spennie, in his time, had extracted small loans from most of his male acquaintances, rarely repaying the same. He had a tendency to forget that he had borrowed half-a-crown here to pay a cab and ten shillings there to settle up for a dinner; and his memory was not much more retentive of larger sums. This made his friends somewhat wary. The consequence was that the great treasure-hunt was a failure from start to finish. He got friendly smiles. He got honeyed apologies. He got earnest assurances of good-will. But he got no money, except from Jimmy Pitt.

He had approached Jimmy in the early stages of the hunt; and Jimmy, being in the mood when he would have loaned anything to anybody, yielded the required five pounds without a murmur.

But what was five pounds? The garment of gloom and the intellectual pallor were once more prominent when his lordship repaired to his room to don the loud tweeds which, as Lord Herbert, he was to wear in the first act.

There is a good deal to be said against stealing, as a habit; but it cannot be denied that, in certain circumstances, it offers an admirable solution of a financial difficulty, and, if the penalties were not so exceedingly unpleasant, it is probable that it would become far more fashionable than it is.

His lordship's mind did not turn immediately to this outlet from his embarrassment. He had never stolen before, and it did not occur to him directly to do so now. There is a conservative strain in all of us. But, gradually, as it was borne in upon him that it was the only course possible, unless he were to grovel before Hargate on the morrow and ask for time to pay - an unthinkable alternative - he found himself contemplating the possibility of having to secure the money by unlawful means. By the time he had finished his theatrical toilet, he had definitely decided that this was the only thing to be done.

His plan was simple. He knew where the money was, in the dressing-table in Sir Thomas's room. He had heard Saunders instructed to put it there. What could be easier than to go and get it? Everything was in his favor. Sir Thomas would be downstairs, receiving his guests. The coast would be clear. Why, it was like finding the money.

Besides, he reflected, as he worked his way through the bottle of Mumm's which he had had the forethought to abstract from the supper-table as a nerve-steadier, it wasn't really stealing. Dash it all, the man had given him the money! It was his own! He had half a mind--he poured himself out another glass of the elixir - to give Sir Thomas a jolly good talking-to into the bargain. Yes, dash it all!

He shot his cuffs fiercely. The British Lion was roused.

A man's first crime is, as a rule, a shockingly amateurish affair. Now and then, it is true, we find beginners forging with the accuracy of old hands, or breaking into houses with the finish of experts. But these are isolated cases. The average tyro lacks generalship altogether. Spennie Dreever may be cited as a typical novice. It did not strike him that inquiries might be instituted by Sir Thomas, when he found the money gone, and that suspicion might conceivably fall upon himself. Courage may be born of champagne, but rarely prudence.

The theatricals began at half-past eight with a duologue. The audience had been hustled into their seats, happier than is usual in such circumstances, owing to the rumor which had been circulated that the proceedings were to terminate with an informal dance. The castle was singularly well constructed for such a purpose. There was plenty of room, and a sufficiency of retreat for those who sat out, in addition to a conservatory large enough to have married off half the couples in the county.

Spennie's idea had been to establish an alibi by mingling with the throng for a few minutes, and then to get through his burglarious specialty during the duologue, when his absence would not be noticed. It might be that, if he disappeared later in the evening, people would wonder what had become of him.

He lurked about until the last of the audience had taken their seats. As he was moving off through the hall, a hand fell upon his shoulder. Conscience makes cowards of us all. Spennie bit his tongue and leaped three inches into the air.

"Hello, Charteris!" he said, gaspingly.

Charteris appeared to be in a somewhat overwrought condition. Rehearsals had turned him into a pessimist, and, now that the actual moment of production had arrived, his nerves were in a thoroughly jumpy condition, especially as the duologue was to begin in two minutes and the obliging person who had undertaken to prompt had disappeared.

"Spennie," said Charteris, "where are you off to?"

"What - what do you mean? I was just going upstairs."

"No, you don't. You've got to come and prompt. That devil Blake has vanished. I'll wring his neck! Come along."

Spennie went, reluctantly. Half-way through the duologue, the official prompter returned with the remark that he had been having a bit of a smoke on the terrace, and that his watch had gone wrong. Leaving him to discuss the point with Charteris, Spennie slipped quietly away.

The delay, however, had had the effect of counteracting the uplifting effects of the Mumm's. The

British Lion required a fresh fillip. He went to his room to administer it. By the time he emerged, he was feeling just right for the task in hand. A momentary doubt occurred to him as to whether it would not be a good thing to go down and pull Sir Thomas' nose as a preliminary to the proceedings; but he put the temptation aside. Business before pleasure.

With a jaunty, if somewhat unsteady, step, he climbed the stairs to the floor above, and made his way down the corridor to Sir Thomas's room. He switched on the light, and went to the dressing-table. The drawer was locked, but in his present mood Spennie, like Love, laughed at locksmiths. He grasped the handle, and threw his weight into a sudden tug. The drawer came out with a report like a pistol-shot.

"There!" said his lordship, wagging his head severely.

In the drawer lay the four bank-notes. The sight of them brought back his grievance with a rush. He would teach Sir Thomas to treat him like a kid! He would show him!

He was removing the notes, frowning fiercely the while, when he heard a cry of surprise from behind him.

He turned, to see Molly. She was still dressed in the evening gown she had worn at dinner; and her eyes were round with wonder. A few moments earlier, as she was seeking her room in order to change her costume for the theatricals, she had almost reached the end of the corridor that led to the landing, when she observed his lordship, flushed of face and moving like some restive charger, come curvetting out of his bedroom in a dazzling suit of tweeds, and make his way upstairs. Ever since their mutual encounter with Sir Thomas before dinner, she had been hoping for a chance of seeing Spennie alone. She had not failed to notice his depression during the meal, and her good little heart had been troubled by the thought that she must have been responsible for it. She knew that, for some reason, what she had said about the letter had brought his lordship into his uncle's bad books, and she wanted to find him and say she was sorry.

Accordingly, she had followed him. His lordship, still in the war-horse vein, had made the pace upstairs too hot, and had disappeared while she was still halfway up. She had arrived at the top just in time to see him turn down the passage into Sir Thomas's dressing-room. She could not think what his object might be. She knew that Sir Thomas was downstairs, so it could not be from the idea of a chat with him that Spennie was seeking the dressing-room.

Faint, yet pursuing, she followed on his trail, and arrived in the doorway just as the pistol-report of the burst lock rang out. She stood looking at him blankly. He was holding a drawer in one hand. Why, she could not imagine.

"Lord Dreever!" she exclaimed.

The somber determination of his lordship's face melted into a twisted, but kindly smile.

"Good!" he said, perhaps a trifle thickly. "Good! Glad you've come. We're pals. You said so - on stairs - b'fore dinner. Very glad you've come. Won't you sit down?"

He waved the drawer benevolently, by way of making her free of the room. The movement disturbed one of the bank-notes, which fluttered in Molly's direction, and fell at her feet.

She stooped and picked it up. When she saw what it was, her bewilderment increased.

"But - but - " she said.

His lordship beamed - upon her with a pebble-beached smile of indiscribable good-will.

"Sit down," he urged. "We're pals. - No quol with you. You're good friend. Quol - Uncle Thomas."

"But, Lord Dreever, what are you doing? What was that noise I heard?"

"Opening drawer," said his lordship, affably.

"But - " she looked again at what she had in her hand - "but this is a five-pound note."

"Five-pound note," said his lordship. "Quite right. Three more of them in here."

Still, she could not understand.

"But - were you - stealing them?"

His lordship drew himself up.

"No," he said, "no, not stealing, no!"

"Then - ?"

"Like this. Before dinner. Old boy friendly as you please - couldn't do enough for me. Touched him for twenty of the best, and got away with it. So far, all well. Then, met you on stairs. You let cat out of bag."

"But why - ? Surely - !"

His lordship gave the drawer a dignified wave.

"Not blaming you," he said, magnanimously. "Not your fault; misfortune. You didn't know. About letter."

"About the letter?" said Molly. "Yes, what was the trouble about the letter? I knew something was wrong directly I had said that I wrote it."

"Trouble was," said his lordship, "that old boy thought it was love-letter. Didn't undeceive him."

"You didn't tell him? Why?"

His lordship raised his eyebrows.

"Wanted touch him twenty of the best," he explained, simply.

For the life of her, Molly could not help laughing.

"Don't laugh," protested his lordship, wounded. "No joke. Serious. Honor at stake."

He removed the three notes, and replaced the drawer.

"Honor of the Dreevers!" he added, pocketing the money.

Molly was horrified.

"But, Lord Dreever!" she cried. "You can't! You musn't! You can't be going, really, to take that money! It's stealing! It isn't yours! You must put it back."

His lordship wagged a forefinger very solemnly at her.

"That," he said, "is where you make error! Mine! Old boy gave them to me."

"Gave them to you? Then, why did you break open the drawer?"

"Old boy took them back again - when he found out about letter."

"Then, they don't belong to you."

"Yes. Error! They do. Moral right."

Molly wrinkled her forehead in her agitation. Men of Lord Dreever's type appeal to the motherly instinct of women. As a man, his lordship was a negligible quantity. He did not count. But as a willful child, to be kept out of trouble, he had a claim on Molly.

She spoke soothingly.

"But, Lord Dreever, - " she began. "Call me Spennie," he urged. "We're pals. You said so - on stairs. Everybody calls me Spennie - even Uncle Thomas. I'm going to pull his nose," he broke off suddenly, as one recollecting a forgotten appointment.

"Spennie, then," said Molly. "You mustn't, Spennie.

You mustn't, really. You - "

"You look rippin' in that dress," said his lordship, irrelevantly.

"Thank you, Spennie, dear. But listen." Molly spoke as if she were humoring a rebellious infant. "You really mustn't take that money. You must put it back. See, I'm putting this note back. Give me the others, and I'll put them in the drawer, too. Then, we'll shut the drawer, and nobody will know."

She took the notes from him, and replaced them in the drawer. He watched her thoughtfully, as if he were pondering the merits of her arguments.

"No," he said, suddenly, "no! Must have them! Moral right. Old boy - "

She pushed him gently away.

"Yes, yes, I know," she said. "I know. It's a shame that you can't have them. But you mustn't take them. Don't you see that he would suspect you the moment he found they were gone, and then you'd get into trouble?"

"Something in that," admitted his lordship.

"Of course there is, Spennie, dear. I'm so glad you see! There they all are, safe again in the drawer. Now, we can go downstairs again, and - "

She stopped. She had closed the door earlier in the proceedings, but her quick ear caught the sound of a footstep in the passage outside.

"Quick!" she whispered, taking his hand and darting to the electric-light switch. "Somebody's coming. We mustn't be caught here. They'd see the broken, drawer, and you'd get into awful trouble. Quick!"

She pushed him behind the curtain where the clothes hung, and switched off the light.

From behind the curtain came the muffled voice of his lordship.

"It's Uncle Thomas. I'm coming out. Pull his nose."

"Be quiet!"

She sprang to the curtain, and slipped noiselessly behind it.

"But, I say - !" began his lordship.

"Hush!" She gripped his arm. He subsided.

The footsteps had halted outside the door. Then, the handle turned softly. The door opened, and closed again with hardly a sound.

The footsteps passed on into the room.

CHAPTER XXV

EXPLANATIONS

Jimmy, like his lordship, had been trapped at the beginning of the duologue, and had not been able to get away till it was nearly over. He had been introduced by Lady Julia to an elderly and adhesive baronet, who had recently spent ten days in New York, and escape had not been won without a struggle. The baronet on his return to England had published a book, entitled, "Modern America and Its People," and it was with regard to the opinions expressed in this volume that he invited Jimmy's views. He had no wish to see the duologue, and it was only after the loss of much precious time that Jimmy was enabled to tear himself away on the plea of having to dress. He cursed the authority on "Modern America and Its People" freely, as he ran upstairs. While the duologue was in progress, there had been no chance of Sir Thomas taking it into his head to visit his dressing-room. He had been, as his valet-detective had observed to Mr. Galer, too busy jollying along the swells. It would be the work of a few moments only to restore the necklace to its place. But for the tenacity of the elderly baronet, the thing would have been done by this time. Now, however, there was no knowing what might not happen. Anybody might come along the passage, and see him. He had one point in his favor. There was no likelihood of the jewels being required by their owner till the conclusion of the theatricals. The part that Lady Julia had been persuaded by Charteris to play mercifully contained no scope for the display of gems.

Before going down to dinner, Jimmy had locked the necklace in a drawer. It was still there, Spike having been able apparently to resist the temptation of recapturing it. Jimmy took it, and went into the corridor. He looked up and down. There was nobody about. He shut his door, and walked quickly in the direction of the dressing-room.

He had provided himself with an electric pocket-torch, equipped with a reflector, which he was in the habit of carrying when on his travels. Once inside, having closed the door, he set this aglow, and looked about him.

Spike had given him minute directions as to the position of the jewel-box. He found it without difficulty. To his untrained eye, it seemed tolerably massive and impregnable, but Spike had evidently known how to open it without much difficulty. The lid was shut, but it came up without an effort when he tried to raise it, and he saw that the lock had been broken.

"Spike's coming on!" he said.

He was dangling the necklace over the box, preparatory to dropping it in, when there was a quick rustle at the other side of the room. The curtain was plucked aside, and Molly came out.

"Jimmy!" she cried.

Jimmy's nerves were always in pretty good order, but at the sight of this apparition he visibly jumped.

"Great Scott!" he said.

The curtain again became agitated by some unseen force, violently this time, and from its depths a plaintive voice made itself heard.

"Dash it all," said the voice, "I've stuck!"

There was another upheaval, and his lordship emerged, his yellow locks ruffled and upstanding, his face crimson.

"Caught my head in a coat or something," he explained at large. "Hullo, Pitt!"

Pressed rigidly against the wall, Molly had listened with growing astonishment to the movements on the other side of the curtain. Her mystification deepened every moment. It seemed to her that the room was still in darkness. She could hear the sound of breathing; and then the light of the torch caught her eye. Who could this be, and why had he not switched on the regular room lights?

She strained her ears to catch a sound. For a while, she heard nothing except the soft breathing. Then came a voice that she knew well; and, abandoning her hiding-place, she came out into the room, and found Jimmy standing, with the torch in his hand, over some dark object in the corner of the room.

It was a full minute after Jimmy's first exclamation of surprise before either of them spoke again. The light of the torch hurt Molly's eyes. She put up a hand, to shade them. It seemed to her that they had been standing like this for years.

Jimmy had not moved. There was something in his attitude that filled Molly with a vague fear. In the shadow behind the torch, he looked shapeless and inhuman.

"You're hurting my eyes," she said, at last.

"I'm sorry," said Jimmy. "I didn't think. Is that better?" He turned the light from her face. Something in his voice and the apologetic haste with which he moved the torch seemed to relax the strain of the situation. The feeling of stunned surprise began to leave her. She found herself thinking coherently again.

The relief was but momentary. Why was Jimmy in the room at that time? Why had he a torch? What had he been doing? The questions shot from her brain like sparks from an anvil.

The darkness began to tear at her nerves. She felt along the wall for the switch, and flooded the whole room with light.

Jimmy laid down the torch, and stood for a moment, undecided. He had concealed the necklace behind him. Now, he brought it forward, and dangled it silently before the eyes of Molly and his lordship. Excellent as were his motives for being in. that room with the necklace in his hand, he could not help feeling, as he met Molly's startled gaze, quite as guilty as if his intentions had been altogether different.

His lordship, having by this time pulled himself together to some extent, was the first to speak.

"I say, you know, what ho!" he observed, not without emotion. "What?"

Molly drew back.

"Jimmy! You were - oh, you can't have been!"

"Looks jolly like it!" said his lordship, judicially.

"I wasn't," said Jimmy. "I was putting them back."

"Putting them back?"

"Pitt, old man," said his lordship solemnly, "that sounds a bit thin."

"Dreever, old man," said Jimmy. "I know it does. But it's the truth."

His lordship's manner became kindly.

"Now, look here, Pitt, old son," he said, "there's nothing to worry about. We're all pals here. You can pitch it straight to us. We won't give you away. We - "

"Be quiet!" cried Molly. "Jimmy!"

Her voice was strained. She spoke with an effort. She was suffering torments. The words her father had said to her on the terrace were pouring back into her mind. She seemed to hear his voice now, cool and confident, warning her against Jimmy, saying that he was crooked. There was a curious whirring in her head.

Everything in the room was growing large and misty. She heard Lord Dreever begin to say something that sounded as if someone were speaking at the end of a telephone; and, then, she was aware that Jimmy was holding her in his arms, and calling to Lord Dreever to bring water,

"When a girl goes like that," said his lordship with an insufferable air of omniscience, "you want to cut her - "

"Come along!" said Jimmy. "Are you going to be a week getting that water?"

His lordship proceeded to soak a sponge without further parley; but, as he carried his dripping burden across the room, Molly recovered. She tried weakly to free herself.

Jimmy helped her to a chair. He had dropped the necklace on the floor, and Lord Dreever nearly trod on it.

"What ho!" observed his lordship, picking it up. "Go easy with the jewelry!"

Jimmy was bending over Molly. Neither of them seemed to be aware of his lordship's presence. Spennie was the sort of person whose existence is apt to be forgotten. Jimmy had had a flash of intuition. For the first time, it had occurred to him that Mr. McEachern might have hinted to Molly something of his own suspicions.

"Molly, dear," he said, "it isn't what you think. I can explain everything. Do you feel better now? Can you listen? I can explain everything."

"Pitt, old boy," protested his lordship, "you don't understand. We aren't going to give you away. We're all - "

Jimmy ignored him.

"Molly, listen," he said.

She sat up.

"Go on, Jimmy," she said.

"I wasn't stealing the necklace. I was putting it back. The man who came to the castle with me, Spike Mullins, took it this afternoon, and brought it to me."

Spike Mullins! Molly remembered the name.

"He thinks I am a crook, a sort of Raffles. It was my fault. I was a fool. It all began that night in New York, when we met at your house. I had been to the opening performance of a play called, 'Love, the Cracksman,' one of those burglar plays."

"Jolly good show," interpolated his lordship, chattily. "It was at the Circle over here. I went twice."

"A friend of mine, a man named Mifflin, had been playing the hero in it, and after the show, at the club, he started in talking about the art of burglary - he'd been studying it - and I said that anybody could burgle a house. And, in another minute, it somehow happened that I had made a bet that I would do it that night. Heaven knows whether I ever really meant to; but, that

P.G. Wodehouse

same night, this man Mullins broke into my flat, and I caught him. We got into conversation, and I worked off on him a lot of technical stuff I'd heard from this actor friend of mine, and he jumped to the conclusion that I was an expert. And, then, it suddenly occurred to me that it would be a good joke on Mifflin if I went out with Mullins, and did break into a house. I wasn't in the mood to think what a fool I was at the time. Well, anyway, we went out, and - well, that's how it all happened. And, then, I met Spike in London, down and out, and brought him here."

He looked at her anxiously. It did not need his lordship's owlish expression of doubt to tell him how weak his story must sound. He had felt it even as he was telling it. He was bound to admit that, if ever a story rang false in every sentence, it was this one.

"Pitt, old man," said his lordship, shaking his head, more in sorrow than in anger, "it won't do, old top. What's the point of putting up any old yarn like that? Don't you see, what I mean is, it's not as if we minded. Don't I keep telling you we're all pals here? I've often thought what a jolly good feller old Raffles was. Regular sportsman! I don't blame a chappie for doing the gentleman burglar touch. Seems to me it's a dashed sporting - "

Molly turned on him suddenly, cutting short his views on the ethics of gentlemanly theft in a blaze of indignation.

"What do you mean?" she cried. "Do you think I don't believe every word Jimmy has said?"

His lordship jumped.

"Well, don't you know, it seemed to me a bit thin. What I mean is - " He met Molly's eye. "Oh, well!" he concluded, lamely.

Molly turned to Jimmy.

"Jimmy, of course, I believe you. I believe every word."

"Molly!"

His lordship looked on, marveling. The thought crossed his mind that he had lost the ideal wife. A girl who would believe any old yarn a feller cared to - If it hadn't been for Katie! For a moment, he felt almost sad.

Jimmy and Molly were looking at each other in silence. From the expression on their faces, his lordship gathered that his existence had once more been forgotten. He saw her hold out her hands to Jimmy, and it seemed to him that the time had come to look away. It was embarrassing for a chap! He looked away.

The next moment, the door opened and closed again, and she had gone.

He looked at Jimmy. Jimmy was still apparently unconscious of his presence.

His lordship coughed.

"Pitt, old man - "

"Hullo!" said Jimmy, coming out of his thoughts with

a start. "You still here? By the way - " he eyed Lord Dreever curiously - "I never thought of asking before - what on earth are you doing here? Why were you behind the curtain? Were you playing hide-and-seek?"

His lordship was not one of those who invent circumstantial stories easily on the spur of the moment. He searched rapidly for something that would pass muster, then abandoned the hopeless struggle. After all, why not be frank? He still believed Jimmy to be of the class of the hero of "Love, the Cracksman." There would be no harm in confiding in him. He was a good fellow, a kindred soul, and would sympathize.

"It's like this," he said. And, having prefaced his narrative with the sound remark that he had been a bit of an ass, he gave Jimmy a summary of recent events.

"What!" said Jimmy. "You taught Hargate picquet? Why, my dear man, he was playing picquet like a professor when you were in short frocks. He's a wonder at it."

His lordship started.

"How's that?" he said. "You don't know him, do you?"

"I met him in New York, at the Strollers' Club. A pal of mine, an actor, this fellow Mifflin I mentioned just now, put him up as a guest. He coined money at picquet. And there were some pretty useful players in the place, too. I don't wonder you found him a promising pupil."

"Then - then - why, dash it, then he's a bally sharper!"

"You're a genius at crisp description," said Jimmy. "You've got him summed up to rights first shot."

"I sha'n't pay him a bally penny!"

"Of course not. If he makes any objection, refer him to me."

His lordship's relief was extreme. The more over-powering effects of the elixir had passed away, and he saw now, what he had not seen in his more exuberant frame of mind, the cloud of suspicion that must have hung over him when the loss of the banknotes was discovered.

He wiped his forehead.

"By Jove!" he said. "That's something off my mind! By George, I feel like a two-year-old. I say, you're a dashed good sort, Pitt."

"You flatter me," said Jimmy. "I strive to please."

"I say, Pitt, that yarn you told us just now - the bet, and all that. Honestly, you don't mean to say that was true, was it? I mean - By Jove! I've got an idea."

"We live in stirring times!"

"Did you say your actor pal's name was Mifflin?" He broke off suddenly before Jimmy could answer. "Great Scott!" he whispered. "What's that! Good lord! Somebody's coming!"

He dived behind the curtain, like a rabbit. The drapery had only just ceased to shake when the door opened, and Sir Thomas Blunt walked in.

CHAPTER XXVI

STIRRING TIMES FOR SIR THOMAS

For a man whose intentions toward the jewels and their owner were so innocent, and even benevolent, Jimmy was in a singularly compromising position. It would have been difficult even under more favorable conditions to have explained to Sir Thomas's satisfaction his presence in the dressing-room. As things stood, it was even harder, for his lordship's last action before seeking cover had been to fling the necklace from him like a burning coal. For the second time in ten minutes, it had fallen to the carpet, and it was just as Jimmy straightened himself after picking it up that Sir Thomas got a full view of him.

The knight stood in the doorway, his face expressing the most lively astonishment. His bulging eyes were fixed upon the necklace in Jimmy's hand. Jimmy could see him struggling to find words to cope with so special a situation, and felt rather sorry for him. Excitement of this kind was bad for a short-necked man of Sir Thomas's type.

With kindly tact, he endeavored to help his host out.

"Good-evening," he said, pleasantly.

P.G. Wodehouse

Sir Thomas stammered. He was gradually nearing speech.

"What - what - what - " he said.

"Out with it," said Jimmy.

" - what - "

"I knew a man once in South Dakota who stammered," said Jimmy. "He used to chew dog-biscuit while he was speaking. It cured him - besides being nutritious. Another good way is to count ten while you're thinking what to say, and then get it out quick."

"You - you blackguard!"

Jimmy placed the necklace carefully on the dressing-table. Then, he turned to Sir Thomas, with his hands thrust into his pockets. Over the knight's head, he could see the folds of the curtain quivering gently, as if stirred by some zephyr. Evidently, the drama of the situation was not lost on Hildebrand Spencer, twelfth Earl of Dreever.

Nor was it lost on Jimmy. This was precisely the sort of situation that appealed to him. He had his plan of action clearly mapped out. He knew that it would be useless to tell the knight the true facts of the case. Sir Thomas was as deficient in simple faith as in Norman blood. Though a Londoner by birth, he had one, at least, of the characteristic traits of the natives of Missouri.

To all appearances, this was a tight corner, but Jimmy fancied that he saw his way out of it. Meanwhile, the situation appealed to him. Curiously enough, it was almost identical with the big scene in act three of "Love, the Cracksman," in which Arthur Mifflin had made such a hit as the debonair burglar.

Jimmy proceeded to give his own idea of what the rendering of a debonair burglar should be. Arthur Mifflin had lighted a cigarette, and had shot out smoke-rings and repartee alternately. A cigarette would have been a great help here, but Jimmy prepared to do his best without properties.

"So - so, it's you, is it?" said Sir Thomas.

"Who told you?"

"Thief! Low thief!"

"Come, now," protested Jimmy. "Why low? Just because you don't know me over here, why scorn me? How do you know I haven't got a big American reputation? For all you can tell, I may be Boston Billie or Sacramento Sam, or someone. Let us preserve the decencies of debate."

"I had my suspicions of you. I had my suspicions from the first, when I heard that my idiot of a nephew had made a casual friend in London. So, this was what you were! A thief, who - "

"I don't mind, personally," interrupted Jimmy, "but I hope, if ever you mix with cracksmen, you won't go calling them thieves. They are frightfully sensitive. You see! There's a world of difference between the two branches of the profession and a good deal of snobbish caste-prejudice. Let us suppose that you were an actor

-manager. How would you enjoy being called a super? You see the idea, don't you? You'd hurt their feelings. Now, an ordinary thief would probably use violence in a case like this. But violence, except in extreme cases - I hope this won't be one of them - is contrary, I understand, to cracksman's etiquette. On the other hand, Sir Thomas, candor compels me to add that I have you covered."

There was a pipe in the pocket of his coat. He thrust the stem earnestly against the lining. Sir Thomas eyed the protuberance apprehensively, and turned a little pale. Jimmy was scowling ferociously. Arthur Mifflin's scowl in act three had been much admired.

"My gun," said Jimmy, "is, as you see, in my pocket. I always shoot from the pocket, in spite of the tailor's bills. The little fellow is loaded and cocked. He's pointing straight at your diamond solitaire. That fatal spot! No one has ever been hit in the diamond solitaire, and survived. My finger is on the trigger. So, I should recommend you not to touch that bell you are looking at. There are other reasons why you shouldn't, but those I will go into presently."

Sir Thomas's hand wavered.

"Do if you like, of course," said Jimmy, agreeably. "It's your own house. But I shouldn't. I am a dead shot at a yard and a half. You wouldn't believe the number of sitting haystacks I've picked off at that distance. I just can't miss. On second thoughts, I sha'n't fire to kill you. Let us be humane on this joyful occasion. I shall just smash your knees. Painful, but not fatal."

He waggled the pipe suggestively. Sir Thomas

blenched. His hand fell to his side.

"Great!" said Jimmy. "After all, why should you be in a hurry to break up this very pleasant little meeting. I'm sure I'm not. Let us chat. How are the theatricals going? Was the duologue a success? Wait till you see our show. Three of us knew our lines at the dress-rehearsal."

Sir Thomas had backed away from the bell, but the retreat was merely for the convenience of the moment. He understood that it might be injudicious to press the button just then; but he had recovered his composure by this time, and he saw that ultimately the game must be his. His face resumed its normal hue. Automatically, his hands began to move toward his coat-tails, his feet to spread themselves. Jimmy noted with a smile these signs of restored complacency. He hoped ere long to upset that complacency somewhat.

Sir Thomas addressed himself to making Jimmy's poition clear to him.

"How, may I ask," he said, "do you propose to leave the castle?"

"Won't you let me have the automobile?" said Jimmy. "But I guess I sha'n't be leaving just yet."

Sir Thomas laughed shortly.

"No," he said - "no! I fancy not. I am with you there!"

"Great minds," said Jimmy. "I shouldn't be surprised if we thought alike on all sorts of subjects. Just think how you came round to my views on ringing bells. But what made you fancy that I intended to leave the castle?"

"I should hardly have supposed that you would be anxious to stay."

"On the contrary! It's the one place I have been in, in the last two years, that I have felt really satisfied with. Usually, I want to move on after a week. But I could stop here forever."

"I am afraid, Mr. Pitt - By the way, an alias, of course?"

Jimmy shook his head.

"I fear not," he said. "If I had chosen an alias, it would have been Tressilyan, or Trevelyan, or something. I call Pitt a poor thing in names. I once knew a man called Ronald Cheylesmore. Lucky devil!"

Sir Thomas returned to the point on which he had been about to touch.

"I am afraid, Mr. Pitt," he said, "that you hardly realize your position."

"No?" said Jimmy, interested.

"I find you in the act of stealing my wife's necklace - "

"Would there be any use in telling you that I was not stealing it, but putting it back?"

Sir Thomas raised his eyebrows in silence.

"No?" said Jimmy. "I was afraid not. You were saying - ?"

"I find you in the act of stealing my wife's necklace," proceeded Sir Thomas, "and, because for the moment you succeed in postponing arrest by threatening me with a revolver - "

An agitated look came into Jimmy's face.

"Great Scott!" he cried. He felt hastily in his pocket.

"Yes," he said; "as I had begun to fear. I owe you an apology, Sir Thomas," he went on with manly dignity, producing the briar, "I am entirely to blame. How the mistake arose I cannot imagine, but I find it isn't a revolver after all."

Sir Thomas' cheeks took on a richer tint of purple. He glared dumbly at the pipe.

"In the excitement of the moment, I guess - " began Jimmy.

Sir Thomas interrupted. The recollection of his needless panic rankled within him.

"You - you - you - "

"Count ten!"

"You - what you propose to gain by this buffoonery, I am at a loss - "

"How can you say such savage things!" protested Jimmy. "Not buffoonery! Wit! Esprit! Flow of soul such as circulates daily in the best society."

Sir Thomas almost leaped toward the bell. With his finger on it, he turned to deliver a final speech.

"I believe you're insane," he cried, "but I'll have no more of it. I have endured this foolery long enough. I'll-"

"Just one moment," said Jimmy. "I said just now that there were reasons besides the revol - well, pipe - why you should not ring that bell. One of them is that all the servants will be in their places in the audience, so that there won't be anyone to answer it. But that's not the most convincing reason. Will you listen to one more before getting busy?"

"I see your game. Don't imagine for a moment that you can trick me."

"Nothing could be further - "

"You fancy you can gain time by talking, and find some way to escape - "

"But I don't want to escape. Don't you realize that in about ten minutes I am due to play an important part in a great drama on the stage?"

"I'll keep you here, I tell you. You'll leave this room," said Sir Thomas, grandly, "over my body."

"Steeple-chasing in the home," murmured Jimmy. "No more dull evenings. But listen. Do listen! I won't keep you a minute, and, if you want to - push that bell after I'm through, you may push it six inches into the wall if you like."

"Well," said Sir Thomas, shortly.

"Would you like me to lead gently up to what I want to say, gradually preparing you for the reception of the news, or shall I - ?"

The knight took out his watch.

"I shall give you one minute," he said.

"Heavens, I must hustle! How many seconds have I got now?"

"If you have anything to say, say it."

"Very well, then," said Jimmy. "It's only this: That necklace is a fraud. The diamonds aren't diamonds at all. They're paste!"

CHAPTER XXVII

A DECLARATION OF INDEPENDENCE

If Jimmy had entertained any doubts concerning the effectiveness of this disclosure, they would have vanished at the sight of the other's face. Just as the rich hues of a sunset pale slowly into an almost imperceptible green, so did the purple of Sir Thomas's cheeks become, in stages, first a dull red, then pink, and finally take on a uniform pallor. His mouth hung open. His attitude of righteous defiance had crumpled. Unsuspected creases appeared in his clothes. He had the appearance of one who has been caught in the machinery.

Jimmy was a little puzzled. He had expected to check the enemy, to bring him to reason, but not to demolish him in this way. There was something in this which he did not understand. When Spike had handed him the stones, and his trained eye, after a moment's searching examination, had made him suspicious, and when, finally, a simple test had proved his suspicions correct, he was comfortably aware that, though found with the necklace on his person, he had knowledge, which, communicated to Sir Thomas, would serve him well. He knew that Lady Julia was not the sort of lady who would bear calmly the announcement that her treasured rope of diamonds was a fraud. He knew enough of her to know that she would demand another necklace, and see that she got it; and that Sir Thomas was not one of those generous and expansive natures which think nothing of an expenditure of twenty thousand pounds.

This was the line of thought that had kept him cheerful during what might otherwise have been a trying interview. He was aware from the first that Sir Thomas would not believe in the purity of his motives; but he was convinced that the knight would be satisfied to secure his silence on the subject of the paste necklace at any price. He had looked forward to baffled rage, furious denunciation, and a dozen other expressions of emotion, but certainly not to collapse of this kind.

The other had begun to make strange, gurgling noises.

"Mind you," said Jimmy, "it's a very good imitation. I'll say that for it. I didn't suspect it till I had the thing in my hands. Looking at it - even quite close - I was taken in for a moment."

Sir Thomas swallowed nervously.

"How did you know?" he muttered.

Again, Jimmy was surprised. He had expected indignant denials and demands for proof, excited reiteration of the statement that the stones had cost twenty thousand pounds.

"How did I know?" he repeated. "If you mean what first made me suspect, I couldn't tell you. It might have been one of a score of things. A jeweler can't say exactly how he gets on the track of fake stones. He can feel them. He can almost smell them. I worked with a jeweler once. That's how I got my knowledge of jewels. But, if you mean, can I prove what I say about this necklace, that's easy. There's no deception. It's simple. See here. These stones are supposed to be diamonds. Well, the diamond is the hardest stone in existence. Nothing will scratch it. Now, I've got a little ruby, out of a college pin, which I know is genuine. By rights, then, that ruby ought not to have scratched these stones. You follow that? But it did. It scratched two of them, the only two I tried. If you like, I can continue the experiment. But there's no need. I can tell you right now what these stones are, I said they were paste, but that wasn't quite accurate. They're a stuff called white jargoon. It's a stuff that's very easily faked. You work it with the flame of a blow-pipe. You don't want a full description, I suppose? Anyway, what happens is that the blow-pipe sets it up like a tonic. Gives it increased specific gravity and a healthy complexion and all sorts of great things of that kind. Two minutes in the flame of a blow-pipe is like a week at the seashore to a bit of white jargoon. Are you satisfied? If it comes to that, I guess you can hardly be expected to be. Convinced is a better word. Are you convinced, or do you hanker after tests like polarized light and refracting liquids?"

Sir Thomas had staggered to a chair.

"So, that was how you knew!" he said.

"That was - " began Jimmy, when a sudden suspicion flashed across his mind. He scrutinized Sir Thomas' pallid face keenly.

"Did you know?" he asked.

He wondered that the possibility had not occurred to

him earlier. This would account for much that had puzzled him in the other's reception of the news. He had supposed, vaguely, without troubling to go far into the probabilities of such a thing, that the necklace which Spike had brought to him had been substituted for the genuine diamonds by a thief. Such things happened frequently, he knew. But, remembering what Molly had told him of the care which Sir Thomas took of this particular necklace, and the frequency with which Lady Julia wore it, he did not see how such a substitution could have been effected. There had been no chance of anybody's obtaining access to these stones for the necessary length of time.

"By George, I believe you did!" he cried. "You must have! So, that's how it happened, is it? I don't wonder it was a shock when I said I knew about the necklace."

"Mr. Pitt!"

"Well?"

"I have something to say to you."

"I'm listening."

Sir Thomas tried to rally. There was a touch of the old pomposity in his manner when he spoke.

"Mr. Pitt, I find you in an unpleasant position - "

Jimmy interrupted.

"Don't you worry about my unpleasant position," he said. "Fix your attention exclusively upon your own. Let us be frank with one another. You're in the cart.

What do you propose to do about it?"

Sir Thomas rallied again, with the desperation of one fighting a lost cause.

"I do not understand you - " he began.

"No?" said Jimmy. "I'll try and make my meaning clear. Correct me from time to time, if I am wrong. The way I size the thing up is as follows: When you married Lady Julia, I gather that it was, so to speak, up to you to some extent. People knew you were a millionaire, and they expected something special in the way of gifts from the bridegroom to the bride. Now, you, being of a prudent and economical nature, began to wonder if there wasn't some way of getting a reputation for lavishness without actually unbelting to any great extent. Am I right?"

Sir Thomas did not answer.

"I am," said Jimmy. "Well, it occurred to you, naturally enough, that a properly-selected gift of jewelry might work the trick. It only needed a little nerve. When you give a present of diamonds to a lady, she is not likely to call for polarized light and refracting liquids and the rest of the circus. In ninety-nine cases out of a hundred, she will take the things on trust. Very well. You trotted off to a jeweler, and put the thing to him confidentially. I guess you suggested paste. But, being a wily person, he pointed out that paste has a habit of not wearing well. It is pretty enough when it's new, but quite a small amount of ordinary wear and tear destroys the polish of the surface and the sharpness of the cutting. It gets scratched easily. Having heard this, and reflecting that Lady Julia was not likely to keep the necklace under a glass case, you rejected paste as too risky. The genial jeweler then suggested white jargoon, mentioning, as I have done, that, after an application or so of the blow-pipe, it's own mother wouldn't know it. If he was a bit of an antiquary, he probably added that, in the eighteenth century, jargoon stones were supposed to be actually an inferior sort of diamond. What could be more suitable? 'Make it jargoon, dear heart,' you cried joyfully, and all was well. Am I right? I notice that you have not corrected me so far."

Whether or not Sir Thomas would have replied in the affirmative is uncertain. He was opening his mouth to speak, when the curtain at the end of the room heaved, and Lord Dreever burst out like a cannon-ball in tweeds.

The apparition effectually checked any speech that Sir Thomas might have been intending to make. Lying back in his chair, he goggled silently at the new arrival. Even Jimmy, though knowing that his lordship had been in hiding, was taken aback. His attention had become so concentrated on his duel with the knight that he had almost forgotten they had an audience.

His lordship broke the silence.

"Great Scott!" he cried.

Neither Jimmy nor Sir Thomas seemed to consider the observation unsound or inadequate. They permitted it to pass without comment.

"You old scoundrel!" added his lordship, addressing Sir Thomas. "And you're the man who called me a welsher!" There were signs of a flicker of spirit in the knight's prominent eyes, but they died away. He made no reply.

"Great Scott!" moaned his lordship, in a fervor of self-pity. "Here have I been all these years letting you give me Hades in every shape and form, when all the while - My goodness, if I'd only known earlier!"

He turned to Jimmy.

"Pitt, old man," he said warmly, "I - dash it! I don't know what to say. If it hadn't been for you - I always did like Americans. I always thought it bally rot that that fuss happened in - in - whenever it was. If it hadn't been for fellows like you," he continued, addressing Sir Thomas once more, "there wouldn't have been any of that frightful Declaration of Independence business. Would there, Pitt, old man?"

These were deep problems, too spacious for casual examination. Jimmy shrugged his shoulders.

"Well, I guess Sir Thomas might not have got along with George Washington, anyway," he said.

"Of course not. Well" - Spennie moved toward the door - "I'm off downstairs to see what Aunt Julia has to say about it all."

A shudder, as if from some electric shock, shook Sir Thomas. He leaped to his feet.

"Spencer," he cried, "I forbid you to say a word to your aunt."
"Oh!" said his lordship. "You do, do you?"

Sir Thomas shivered.

"She would never let me hear the last of it."

"I bet she wouldn't. I'll go and see."

"Stop!"

"Well?"

Sir Thomas dabbed at his forehead with his handkerchief. He dared not face the vision of Lady Julia in possession of the truth. At one time, the fear lest she might discover the harmless little deception he had practised had kept him awake at night, but gradually, as the days went by and the excellence of the imitation stones had continued to impose upon her and upon everyone else who saw them, the fear had diminished. But it had always been at the back of his mind. Even in her calmer moments, his wife was a source of mild terror to him. His imagination reeled at the thought of what depths of aristocratic scorn and indignation she would plumb in a ease like this.

"Spencer," he said, "I insist that you shall not inform your aunt of this!"

"What? You want me to keep my mouth shut? You want me to become an accomplice in this beastly, low-down deception? I like that!"

"The point," said Jimmy, "is well taken. Noblesse oblige, and all that sort of thing. The blood of the Dreevers boils furiously at the idea. Listen! You can hear it sizzling."

Lord Dreever moved a step nearer the door.

"Stop!" cried Sir Thomas again. "Spencer!"

"Well?"

"Spencer, my boy, it occurs to me that perhaps I have not always treated you very well - "

"'Perhaps!' 'Not always!' Great Scott, I'll have a fiver each way on both those. Considering you've treated me like a frightful kid practically ever since you've known me, I call that pretty rich! Why, what about this very night, when I asked you for a few pounds?"

"It was only the thought that you had been gambling - "

"Gambling! How about palming off faked diamonds on Aunt Julia for a gamble?"

"A game of skill, surely?" murmured Jimmy.

"I have been thinking the matter over," said Sir Thomas, "and, if you really need the - was it not fifty pounds?"

"It was twenty," said his lordship. "And I don't need it. Keep it. You'll want all you can save for a new necklace."

His fingers closed on the door-handle.

"Spencer, stop!"

"Well?"

"We must talk this over. We must not be hasty."

Sir Thomas passed the handkerchief over his forehead.

"In the past, perhaps," he resumed, "our relations have not been quite - the fault was mine. I have always endeavored to do my duty. It is a difficult task to look after a young man of your age - "

His lordship's sense of his grievance made him eloquent.

"Dash it all!" he cried. "That's just what I jolly well complain of. Who the dickens wanted you to look after me? Hang it, you've kept your eye on me all these years like a frightful policeman! You cut off my allowance right in the middle of my time at college, just when I needed it most, and I had to come and beg for money whenever I wanted to buy a cigarette. I looked a fearful ass, I can tell you! Men who knew me used to be dashed funny about it. I'm sick of the whole bally business. You've given me a jolly thin time all this while, and now I'm going to get a bit of my own back. Wouldn't you, Pitt, old man?"

Jimmy, thus suddenly appealed to, admitted that, in his lordship's place, he might have experienced a momentary temptation to do something of the kind.

"Of course," said his lordship; "any fellow would."

"But, Spencer, let met - "

"You've soured my life," said his lordship, frowning a tense, Byronic frown. "That's what you've done -

soured my whole bally life. I've had a rotten time. I've had to go about touching my friends for money to keep me going. Why, I owe you a fiver, don't I, Pitt, old man?"

It was a tenner, to be finnickingly accurate about details, but Jimmy did not say so. He concluded, rightly, that the memory of the original five pounds which he had lent Lord Dreever at the Savoy Hotel had faded from the other's mind.

"Don't mention it," he said.

"But I do mention it," protested his lordship, shrilly. "It just proves what I say. If I had had a decent allowance, it wouldn't have happened. And you wouldn't give me enough to set me going in the diplomatic service. That's another thing. Why wouldn't you do that?"

Sir Thomas pulled himself together.

"I hardly thought you qualified, my dear boy - "

His lordship did not actually foam at the mouth, but he looked as if he might do so at any moment. Excitement and the memory of his wrongs, lubricated, as it were, by the champagne he had consumed both at and after dinner, had produced in him a frame of mind far removed from the normal. His manners no longer had that repose which stamps the caste of Vere de Vere. He waved his hands:

"I know, I know!" he shouted. "I know you didn't. You thought me a fearful fool. I tell you, I'm sick of it. And always trying to make me marry money! Dashed humiliating! If she hadn't been a jolly sensible girl, you'd have spoiled Miss McEachern's life as well as mine. You came very near it. I tell you, I've had enough of it. I'm in love. I'm in love with the rippingest girl in England. You've seen her, Pitt, old top. Isn't she a ripper?"

Jimmy stamped the absent lady with the seal of his approval.

"I tell you, if she'll have me, I'm going to marry her."

The dismay written on every inch of Sir Thomas's countenance became intensified at these terrific words. Great as had been his contempt for the actual holder of the title, considered simply as a young man, he had always been filled with a supreme respect for the Dreever name.

"But, Spencer," he almost howled, "consider your position! You cannot - "

"Can't I, by Jove! If she'll have me! And damn my position! What's my position got to do with it? Katie's the daughter of a general, if it comes to that. Her brother was at college with me. If I'd had a penny to call my own, I'd have asked her to marry me ages ago. Don't you worry about my position!"

Sir Thomas croaked feebly.

"Now, look here," said his lordship, with determination. "Here's the whole thing in a jolly old nutshell. If you want me to forget about this little flutter in fake diamonds of yours, you've got to pull up your socks, and start in to do things. You've got to get me attached to some embassy for a beginning. It won't be difficult.

There's dozens of old boys in London, who knew the governor when he was alive, who will jump at the chance of doing me a good turn. I know I'm a bit of an ass in some ways, but that's expected of you in the diplomatic service. They only want you to wear evening clothes as if you were used to them, and be a bit of a flyer at dancing, and I can fill the bill all right as far as that goes. And you've got to give your jolly old blessing to Katie and me - if she'll have me. That's about all I can think of for the moment. How do we go? Are you on?"

"It's preposterous," began Sir Thomas.

Lord Dreever gave the door-handle a rattle.

"It's a hold-up all right," said Jimmy, soothingly. "I don't want to butt in on a family conclave, but my advice, if asked, would be to unbelt before the shooting begins. You've got something worse than a pipe pointing at you, now. As regards my position in the business, don't worry. My silence is presented gratis. Give me a loving smile, and my lips are sealed."

Sir Thomas turned on the speaker.

"As for you - " he cried.

"Never mind about Pitt," said his lordship. "He's a dashed good fellow, Pitt. I wish there were more like him. And he wasn't pinching the stuff, either. If you had only listened when he tried to tell, you mightn't be in such a frightful hole. He was putting the things back, as he said. I know all about it. Well, what's the answer?"

For a moment, Sir Thomas seemed on the point of refusal. But, just as he was about to speak, his lordship opened the door, and at the movement he collapsed again.

"I will," he cried. "I will!"

"Good," said his lordship with satisfaction. "That's a bargain. Coming downstairs, Pitt, old man? We shall be wanted on the stage in about half a minute."

"As an antidote to stage fright," said Jimmy, as they went along the corridor, "little discussions of that kind may be highly recommended. I shouldn't mind betting that you feel fit for anything?"

"I feel like a two-year-old," assented his lordship, enthusiastically. "I've forgotten all my part, but I don't care. I'll just go on and talk to them."

"That," said Jimmy, "is the right spirit. Charteris will get heart-disease, but it's the right spirit. A little more of that sort of thing, and amateur theatricals would be worth listening to. Step lively, Roscius; the stage waits."

CHAPTER XXVIII

SPENNIE'S HOUR OF CLEAR VISION

Mr. McEachern sat in the billiard-room, smoking. He was alone. From where he sat, he could hear distant strains of music. The more rigorous portion of the evening's entertainment, the theatricals, was over, and the nobility and gentry, having done their duty by sitting through the performance, were now enjoying themselves in the ballroom. Everybody was happy. The play had been quite as successful as the usual amateur performance. The prompter had made himself a great favorite from the start, his series of duets with Spennie having been especially admired; and Jimmy, as became an old professional, had played his part with great finish and certainty of touch, though, like the bloodhounds in "Uncle Tom's Cabin" on the road, he had had poor support. But the audience bore no malice. No collection of individuals is less vindictive than an audience at amateur theatricals. It was all over now. Charteris had literally gibbered in the presence of eye-witnesses at one point in the second act, when Spennie, by giving a wrong cue, had jerked the play abruptly into act three, where his colleagues, dimly suspecting something wrong, but not knowing what it was, had kept it for two minutes, to the mystification of the audience. But, now Charteris had begun to forget. As he two-stepped down the room, the lines of agony on his face were softened. He even smiled.

As for Spennie, the brilliance of his happy grin dazzled all beholders.

He was still wearing it when he invaded the solitude of Mr. McEachern. In every dance, however greatly he may be enjoying it, there comes a time when a man needs a meditative cigarette apart from the throng. It came to Spennie after the seventh item on the program. The billiard-room struck him as admirably suitable in every way. It was not likely to be used as a sitting-out place, and it was near enough to the ball-room to enable him to hear when the music of item number nine should begin.

Mr. McEachern welcomed his visitor. In the turmoil following the theatricals, he had been unable to get a word with any of the persons with whom he most wished to speak. He had been surprised that no announcement of the engagement had been made at the end of the performance. Spennie would be able to supply him with information as to when the announcement might be expected.

Spennie hesitated for an instant when he saw who was in the room. He was not over-anxious for a tete-a-tete with Molly's father just then. But, re-fleeting that, after all, he was not to blame for any disappointment that might be troubling the other, he switched on his grin again, and walked in.

"Came in for a smoke," he explained, by way of opening the conversation. "Not dancing the next."

"Come in, my boy, come in," said Mr. McEachern. "I

was waiting to see you."

Spennie regretted his entrance. He had supposed that the other had heard the news of the breaking-off of the engagement. Evidently, however, McEachern had not. This was a nuisance. The idea of flight came to Spennie, but he dismissed it. As nominal host that night, he had to dance many duty-dances. This would be his only chance of a smoke for hours, and the billiard-room was the best place for it.

He sat down, and lighted a cigarette, casting about the while for an innocuous topic of conversation.

"Like the show?" he inquired.

"Fine," said Mr. McEachern. "By the way - "

Spennie groaned inwardly. He had forgotten that a determined man can change the conversation to any subject he pleases by means of those three words.

"By the way," said Mr. McEachern, "I thought Sir Thomas - wasn't your uncle intending to announce - ?"

"Well, yes, he was," said Spennie.

"Going to do it during the dancing, maybe?"

"Well - er - no. The fact is, he's not going to do it at all, don't you know." Spennie inspected the red end of his cigarette closely. "As a matter of fact, it's kind of broken off."

The other's exclamation jarred on him. Rotten, having to talk about this sort of thing!

"Broken off?"

Spennie nodded.

"Miss McEachern thought it over, don't you know," he said, "and came to the conclusion that it wasn't good enough."

Now that it was said, he felt easier. It had merely been the awkwardness of having to touch on the thing that had troubled him. That his news might be a blow to McEachern did not cross his mind. He was a singularly modest youth, and, though he realized vaguely that his title had a certain value in some persons' eyes, he could not understand anyone mourning over the loss of him as a son-in-law. Katie's father, the old general, thought him a fool, and once, during an attack of gout, had said so. Spennie was wont to accept this as the view which a prospective father-in-law might be expected to entertain regarding himself.

Oblivious, therefore, to the storm raging a yard away from him, he smoked on with great contentment, till suddenly it struck him that, for a presumably devout lover, jilted that very night, he was displaying too little emotion. He debated swiftly within himself whether or not he should have a dash at manly grief, but came to the conclusion that it could not be done. Melancholy on this maddest, merriest day of all the glad New Year, the day on which he had utterly routed the powers of evil, as represented by Sir Thomas, was impossible. He decided, rather, on a let-us-be-reasonable attitude.

"It wouldn't have done, don't you know," he said. "We weren't suited. What I mean to say is, I'm a bit of a dashed sort of silly ass in some ways, if you know

P.G. Wodehouse

what I mean. A girl like Miss McEachern couldn't have been happy with me. She wants one of these capable, energetic fellers."

This struck him as a good beginning - modest, but not groveling. He continued, tapping quite a respectably deep vein of philosophy as he spoke.

"You see, dear old top - I mean, sir, you see, it's like this. As far as women are concerned, fellers are divided into two classes. There's the masterful, capable Johnnies, and the - er - the other sort. Now, I'm the other sort. My idea of the happy married life is to be - well, not exactly downtrodden, but - you know what I mean - kind of second fiddle. I want a wife - " his voice grew soft and dreamy - "who'll pet me a good deal, don't you know, stroke my hair a lot, and all that. I haven't it in me to do the master-in-my-own-house business. For me, the silent-devotion touch. Sleeping on the mat outside her door, don't you know, when she wasn't feeling well, and being found there in the morning and being rather cosseted for my thoughtfulness. That's the sort of idea. Hard to put it quite O. K., but you know the sort of thing I mean. A feller's got to realize his jolly old limitations if he wants to be happy though married, what? Now, suppose Miss McEachern was to marry me! Great Scott, she'd be bored to death in a week. Honest! She couldn't help herself. She wants a chap with the same amount of go in him that she's got."

He lighted another cigarette. He was feeling pleased with himself. Never before had ideas marshaled themselves in his mind in such long and well-ordered ranks. He felt that he could go on talking like this all night. He was getting brainier every minute. He remembered reading in some book somewhere of a girl (or chappie) who had had her (or his) "hour of clear vision." This was precisely what had happened now. Whether it was owing to the excitement of what had taken place that night, or because he had been keying up his thinking powers with excellent dry champagne, he did not know. All he knew was that he felt on top of his subject. He wished he had had a larger audience.

"A girl like Miss McEachern doesn't want any of that hair-stroking business. She'd simply laugh at a feller if he asked for it. She needs a chappie of the get-on-or-get-out type, somebody in the six cylinder class. And, as a matter of fact, between ourselves, I rather think she's found him."

"What!"

Mr. McEachern half rose from his chair. All his old fears had come surging back.

"What do you mean?"

"Fact," said his lordship, nodding. "Mind you, I don't know for certain. As the girl says in the song, I don't know, but I guess. What I mean to say is, they seemed jolly friendly, and all that; calling each other by their first names, and so on."

"Who - ?"

"Pitt," said his lordship. He was leaning back, blowing a smoke-ring at the moment, so he did not see the look on the other's face and the sudden grip of the fingers on the arms of the chair. He went on with some enthusiasm.

P.G. Wodehouse

"Jimmy Pitt!" he said. "Now, there's a feller! Full of oats to the brim, and fairly bursting with go and energy. A girl wouldn't have a dull moment with a chap like that. You know," he proceeded confidently, "there's a lot in this idea of affinities. Take my word for it, dear old - sir. There's a girl up in London, for instance. Now, she and I hit it off most amazingly. There's hardly a thing we don't think alike about. For instance, 'The Merry Widow' didn't make a bit of a hit with her. Nor did it with me. Yet, look at the millions of people who raved about it. And neither of us likes oysters. We're affinities - that's why. You see the same sort of thing all over the place. It's a jolly queer business. Sometimes, makes me believe in re-in-what's-it's-name. You know what I mean. All that in the poem, you know. How does it go? 'When you were a tiddley-om-pom, and I was a thingummajig.' Dashed brainy bit of work. I was reading it only the other day. Well, what I mean to say is, it's my belief that Jimmy Pitt and Miss McEachern are by way of being something in that line. Doesn't it strike you that they are just the sort to get on together? You can see it with half an eye. You can't help liking a feller like Jimmy Pitt. He's a sport! I wish I could tell you some of the things he's done, but I can't, for reasons. But you can take it from me, he's a sport. You ought to cultivate him. You'd like him ... Oh, dash it, there's the music. I must be off. Got to dance this one."

He rose from his chair, and dropped his cigarette into the ash-tray.

"So long," he said, with a friendly nod. "Wish I could stop, but it's no go. That's the last let-up I shall have to-night."

He went out, leaving Mr. McEachern a prey to many and varied emotions.

P.G. Wodehouse

CHAPTER XXIX

THE LAST ROUND

He had only been gone a few minutes when Mr. McEachern's meditations were again interrupted. This time, the visitor was a stranger to him, a dark-faced, clean-shaven man. He did not wear evening clothes, so could not be one of the guests; and Mr. McEachern could not place him immediately. Then, he remembered. He had seen him in Sir Thomas Blunt's dressing-room. This was Sir Thomas's valet.

"Might I have a word with you, sir?"

"What is it?" asked McEachern, staring heavily. His mind had not recovered from the effect of Lord Dreever's philosophical remarks. There was something of a cloud on his brain. To judge from his lordship's words, things had been happening behind his back; and the idea of Molly's deceiving him was too strange to be assimilated in an instant. He looked at the valet dully.

"What is it?" he asked again.

"I must apologize for intruding, but I thought it best to approach you before making my report to Sir Thomas."

"Your report?"

"I am employed by a private inquiry agency."

"What!"

"Yes, sir. Wragge's. You may have heard of us. In Holborn Bars. Very old established. Divorce a specialty. You will have seen the advertisements. Sir Thomas wrote asking for a man, and the governor sent me down. I have been with the house some years. My job, I gathered, was to keep my eyes open generally. Sir Thomas, it seemed, had no suspicions of any definite person. I was to be on the spot just in case, in a manner of speaking. And it's precious lucky I was, or her ladyship's jewels would have been gone. I've done a fair cop this very night."

He paused, and eyed the ex-policeman keenly. McEachern was obviously excited. Could Jimmy have made an attempt on the jewels during the dance? or Spike?

"Say," he said, "was it a red-headed - ?"

The detective was watching him with a curious smile.

"No, he wasn't red-headed. You seem interested, sir. I thought you would be. I will tell you all about it. I had had my suspicions of this party ever since he arrived. And I may say that it struck me at the time that there was something mighty fishy about the way he got into the castle."

McEachern started. So, he had not been the only one to

suspect Jimmy's motives in attaching himself to Lord Dreever.

"Go on," he said.

"I suspected that there was some game on, and it struck me that this would be the day for the attempt, the house being upside down, in a manner of speaking, on account of the theatricals. And I was right. I kept near those jewels on and off all day, and, presently, just as I had thought, along comes this fellow. He'd hardly got to the door when I was on him."

"Good boy! You're no rube."

"We fought for a while, but, being a bit to the good in strength, and knowing something about the game, I had the irons on him pretty quick, and took him off, and locked him in the cellar. That's how it was, sir."

Mr. McEachern's relief was overwhelming. If Lord Dreever's statement was correct and Jimmy had really succeeded in winning Molly's affection, this would indeed be a rescue at the eleventh hour. It was with a Nunc-Dimittis air that he felt for his cigar-case, and extended it toward the detective. A cigar from his own private case was with him a mark of supreme favor and good-will, a sort of accolade which he bestowed only upon the really meritorious few.

Usually, it was received with becoming deference; but on this occasion there was a somewhat startling deviation from routine; for, just as he was opening the case, something cold and hard pressed against each of his wrists, there was a snap and a click, and, looking up, dazed, he saw that the detective had sprung back, and was contemplating him with a grim smile over the barrel of an ugly-looking little revolver.

Guilty or innocent, the first thing a man does when, he finds handcuffs on his wrists is to try to get them off. The action is automatic. Mr. McEachern strained at the steel chain till the veins stood out on his forehead. His great body shook with rage.

The detective eyed these efforts with some satisfaction. The picture presented by the other as he heaved and tugged was that of a guilty man trapped.

"It's no good, my friend," he said.

The voice brought McEachern back to his senses. In the first shock of the thing, the primitive man in him had led him beyond the confines of self-restraint. He had simply struggled unthinkingly. Now, he came to himself again.

He shook his manacled hands furiously.

"What does this mean?" he shouted. "What the - ?"

"Less noise," said the detective, sharply. "Get back!" he snapped, as the other took a step forward.

"Do you know who I am?" thundered McEachern.

"No," said the detective. "And that's just why you're wearing those bracelets. Come, now, don't be a fool. The game's up. Can't you see that?"

McEachern leaned helplessly against the billiard-table. He felt weak. Everything was unreal. Had he gone mad? he wondered.

"That's right," said the detective. "Stay there. You can't do any harm there. It was a pretty little game, I'll admit. You worked it well. Meeting your old friend from New York and all, and having him invited to the castle. Very pretty. New York, indeed! Seen about as much of New York as I have of Timbuctoo. I saw through him."

Some inkling of the truth began to penetrate McEachern's consciousness. He had become obsessed with the idea that, as the captive was not Spike, it must be Jimmy. The possibility of Mr. Galer's being the subject of discussion only dawned upon him now.

"What do you mean?" he cried. "Who is it that you have arrested?"

"Blest if I know. You can tell me that, I should think, seeing he's an old Timbuctoo friend of yours. Galer's the name he goes by here."

"Galer!"

"That's the man. And do you know what he had the impudence, the gall, to tell me? That he was in my own line of business. A detective! He said you had sent for him to come here!"

The detective laughed amusedly at the recollection.

"And so he is, you fool. So I did."

"Oh, you did, did you? And what business had you bringing detectives into other people's houses?"

Mr. McEachern started to answer, but checked himself. Never before had he appreciated to the full the depth and truth of the proverb relating to the frying-pan and the fire. To clear himself, he must mention his suspicions of Jimmy, and also his reasons for those suspicions. And to do that would mean revealing his past. It was Scylla and Charybdis.

A drop of perspiration trickled down his temple.

"What's the good?" said the detective. "Mighty ingenious idea, that, only you hadn't allowed for there being a real detective in the house. It was that chap pitching me that yarn that made me suspicious of you. I put two and two together. 'Partners,' I said to myself. I'd heard all about you, scraping acquaintance with Sir Thomas and all. Mighty ingenious. You become the old family friend, and then you let in your pal. He gets the stuff, and hands it over to you. Nobody dreams of suspecting you, and there you are. Honestly, now, wasn't that the game?"

"It's all a mistake - " McEachern was beginning, when the door-handle turned.

The detective looked over his shoulder. McEachern glared dumbly. This was the crowning blow, that there should be spectators of his predicament.

Jimmy strolled into the room.

"Dreever told me you were in here," he said to McEachern. "Can you spare me a - Hullo!"

The detective had pocketed his revolver at the first sound of the handle. To be discreet was one of the chief articles in the creed of the young men from Wragge's Detective Agency. But handcuffs are not easily concealed. Jimmy stood staring in amazement at McEachern's wrists.

"Some sort of a round game?" he enquired with interest.

The detective became confidential.

"It's this way, Mr. Pitt. There's been some pretty deep work going on here. There's a regular gang of burglars in the place. This chap here's one of them."

"What, Mr. McEachern!"

"That's what he calls himself."

It was all Jimmy could do to keep himself from asking Mr. McEachern whether he attributed his downfall to drink. He contented himself with a sorrowful shake of the head at the fermenting captive. Then, he took up the part of the prisoner's attorney.

"I don't believe it," he said. "What makes you. think so?"

"Why, this afternoon, I caught this man's pal, the fellow that calls himself Galer - "

"I know the man," said Jimmy. "He's a detective, really. Mr. McEachern brought him down here."

The sleuth's jaw dropped limply, as if he had received a blow.

"What?" he said, in a feeble voice.

"Didn't I tell you - ?" began Mr. McEachern; but the sleuth was occupied with Jimmy. That sickening premonition of disaster was beginning to steal over him. Dimly, he began to perceive that he had blundered.

"Yes," said Jimmy. "Why, I can't say; but Mr. McEachern was afraid someone might try to steal Lady Julia Blunt's rope of diamonds. So, he wrote to London for this man, Galer. It was officious, perhaps, but not criminal. I doubt if, legally, you could handcuff a man for a thing like that. What have you done with good Mr. Galer?"

"I've locked him in the coal-cellar," said the detective, dismally. The thought of the interview in prospect with the human bloodhound he had so mishandled was not exhilarating.

"Locked him in the cellar, did you?" said Jimmy. "Well, well, I daresay he's very happy there. He's probably busy detecting black-beetles. Still, perhaps you had better go and let him out. Possibly, if you were to apologize to him - ? Eh? Just as you think. I only suggest. If you want somebody to vouch for Mr. McEachern's non-burglariousness, I can do it. He is a gentleman of private means, and we knew each other out in New York - we are old acquaintances."

"I never thought - "

"That," said Jimmy, with sympathetic friendliness, "if you will allow me to say so, is the cardinal mistake you detectives make. You never do think."

"It never occurred to me - "

The detective looked uneasily at Mr. McEachern. There were indications in the policeman's demeanor that the moment following release would be devoted exclusively to a carnival of violence, with a certain sleuth-hound playing a prominent role.

He took the key of the handcuffs from his pocket, and toyed with it. Mr. McEachern emitted a low growl. It was enough.

"If you wouldn't mind, Mr. Pitt," said the sleuth, obsequiously. He thrust the key into Jimmy's hands, and fled.

Jimmy unlocked the handcuffs. Mr. McEachern rubbed his wrists.

"Ingenious little things," said Jimmy.

"I'm much obliged to you," growled Mr. McEachern, without looking up.

"Not at all. A pleasure. This circumstantial evidence thing is the devil, isn't it? I knew a man who broke into a house in New York to win a bet, and to this day the owner of that house thinks him a professional burglar."

"What's that?" said Mr. McEachern, sharply.

"Why do I say 'a man '? Why am I so elusive and mysterious? You're quite right. It sounds more dramatic, but after all what you want is facts. Very well. I broke into your house that night to win a bet. That's the limpid truth."

McEachern was staring at him. Jimmy proceeded.

"You are just about to ask - what was Spike Mullins doing with me? Well, Spike had broken into my flat an hour before, and I took him along with me as a sort of guide, philosopher, and friend."

"Spike Mullins said you were a burglar from England."

"I'm afraid I rather led him to think so. I had been to see the opening performance of a burglar-play called, 'Love, the Cracksman,' that night, and I worked off on Spike some severely technical information I had received from a pal of mine who played lead in the show. I told you when I came in that I had been talking to Lord Dreever. Well, what he was saying to me was that he had met this very actor man, a fellow called Mifflin - Arthur Mifflin - in London just before he met me. He's in London now, rehearsing for a show that's come over from America. You see the importance of this item? It means that, if you doubt my story, all you need do is to find Mifflin - I forgot what theater his play is coming on at, but you could find out in a second - and ask him to corroborate. Are you satisfied?"

McEachern did not answer. An hour before, he would have fought to the last ditch for his belief in Jimmy's crookedness; but the events of the last ten minutes had shaken him. He could not forget that it was Jimmy who had extricated him from a very uncomfortable position. He saw now that that position was not so bad as it had seemed at the time, for the establishing of the innocence of Mr. Galer could have been effected on the morrow by an exchange of telegrams between the castle and Dodson's Private Inquiry Agency; yet it had certainly been bad enough. But for Jimmy, there would have been several hours of acute embarrassment, if nothing worse. He felt something of a reaction in Jimmy's favor.

Still, it is hard to overcome a deep-rooted prejudice in an instant. He stared doubtfully.

"See here, Mr. McEachern," said Jimmy, "I wish you would listen quietly to me for a minute or two. There's really no reason on earth why we should be at one another's throats in this way. We might just as well be friends. Let's shake, and call the fight off. I guess you know why I came in here to see you?"

McEachern did not speak.

"You know that your daughter has broken off her engagement to Lord Dreever?"

"Then, he was right!" said McEachern, half to himself. "It is you?"

Jimmy nodded. McEachern drummed his fingers on the table, and gazed thoughtfully at him.

"Is Molly - ?" he said at length. "Does Molly - ?"

"Yes," said Jimmy.

McEachern continued his drumming. "Don't think there's been anything underhand about this," said Jimmy. "She absolutely refused to do anything unless you gave your consent. She said you had been partners all her life, and she was going to do the square thing by you."

"She did?" said McEachern, eagerly.

"I think you ought to do the square thing by her. I'm not much, but she wants me. Do the square thing by her."

He stretched out his hand, but he saw that the other did not notice the movement. McEachern was staring straight in front of him. There was a look in his eyes that Jimmy had never seen there before, a frightened, hunted look. The rugged aggressiveness of his mouth and chin showed up in strange contrast. The knuckles of his clenched fists were white.

"It's too late," he burst out. "I'll be square with her now, but it's too late. I won't stand in her way when I can make her happy. But I'll lose her! Oh, my God, I'll lose her!"

He gripped the edge of the table.

"Did you think I had never said to myself," he went on, "the things you said to me that day when we met here? Did you think I didn't know what I was? Who should know it better than myself? But she didn't. I'd kept it from her. I'd sweat for fear she would find out some day. When I came over here, I thought I was safe. And, then, you came, and I saw you together. I thought you were a crook. You were with Mullins in New York. I told her you were a crook."

"You told her that!"

"I said I knew it. I couldn't tell her the truth - why I thought so. I said I had made inquiries in New York, and found out about you."

Jimmy saw now. The mystery was solved. So, that was why Molly had allowed them to force her into the engagement with Dreever. For a moment, a rush of anger filled him; but he looked at McEachern, and it died away. He could not be vindictive now. It would be like hitting a beaten man. He saw things suddenly from the other's view-point, and he pitied him.

"I see," he said, slowly.

McEachern gripped the table in silence.

"I see," said Jimmy again. "You mean, she'll want an explanation."

He thought for a moment.

"You must tell her," he said, quickly. "For your own sake, you must tell her. Go and do it now. Wake up, man!" He shook him by the shoulder. "Go and do it now. She'll forgive you. Don't be afraid of that. Go and look for her, and tell her now."

McEachern roused himself.

"I will," he said.

"It's the only way," said Jimmy.

McEachern opened the door, then fell back a pace. Jimmy could hear voices in the passage outside. He recognized Lord Dreever's.

McEachern continued to back away from the door.

Lord Dreever entered, with Molly on his arm.

"Hullo," said his lordship, looking round. "Hullo, Pitt! Here we all are, what?"

"Lord Dreever wanted to smoke," said Molly.

She smiled, but there was anxiety in her eyes. She looked quickly at her father and at Jimmy.

"Molly, my dear," said McEachern huskily, "I to speak to you for a moment."

Jimmy took his lordship by the arm.

"Come along, Dreever," he said. "You can come and sit out with me. We'll go and smoke on the terrace."

They left the room together.

"What does the old boy want?" inquired his lordship. "Are you and Miss McEachern - ?"

"We are," said Jimmy.

"By Jove, I say, old chap! Million congratulations, and all that sort of rot, you know!"

"Thanks," said Jimmy. "Have a cigarette?"

His lordship had to resume his duties in the ballroom after awhile; but Jimmy sat on, smoking and thinking. The night was very still. Now and then, a sparrow would rustle in the ivy on the castle wall, and somewhere in the distance a dog was barking. The music had begun again in the ball-room. It sounded faint and thin where he sat.

In the general stillness, the opening of the door at the top of the steps came sharply to his ears. He looked up. Two figures were silhouetted for a moment against the light, and then the door closed again. They began to move slowly down the steps.

Jimmy had recognized them. He got up. He was in the shadow. They could not see him. They began to walk down the terrace. They were quite close now. Neither was speaking; but, presently when they were but a few feet away, they stopped. There was the splutter of a match, and McEachern lighted a cigar. In the yellow light, his face was clearly visible. Jimmy looked, and was content.

He edged softly toward the shrubbery at the end of the terrace, and, entering it without a sound, began to make his way back to the house.

CHAPTER XXX

CONCLUSION

The American liner, St. Louis, lay in the Empress Dock at Southampton, taking aboard her passengers. All sorts and conditions of men flowed in an unceasing stream up the gangway.

Leaning over the second-class railing, Jimmy Pitt and Spike Mullins watched them thoughtfully.

Jimmy looked up at the Blue Peter that fluttered from the fore-mast, and then at Spike. The Bowery boy's face was stolid and expressionless. He was smoking a short wooden pipe with an air of detachment.

"Well, Spike," said Jimmy. "Your schooner's on the tide now, isn't it? Your vessel's at the quay. You've got some queer-looking fellow-travelers. Don't miss the two Cingalese sports, and the man in the turban and the baggy breeches. I wonder if they're air-tight. Useful if he fell overboard."

"Sure," said Spike, directing a contemplative eye toward the garment in question. "He knows his business."

"I wonder what those men on the deck are writing.

They've been scribbling away ever since we came here. Probably, society journalists. We shall see in next week's papers: 'Among the second-class passengers, we noticed Mr. "Spike" Mullins, looking as cheery as ever.' It's a pity you're so set on. going, Spike. Why not change your mind, and stop?"

For a moment, Spike looked wistful. Then, his countenance resumed its woodenness. "Dere ain't no use for me dis side, boss," he said. "New York's de spot. Youse don't want none of me, now you're married. How's Miss Molly, boss?"

"Splendid, Spike, thanks. We're going over to France by to-night's boat."

"It's been a queer business," Jimmy continued, after a pause, "a deuced-queer business! Still, I've come very well out of it, at any rate. It seems to me that you're the only one of us who doesn't end happily, Spike. I'm married. McEachern's butted into society so deep that it would take an excavating party with dynamite to get him out of it. Molly - well, Molly's made a bad bargain, but I hope she won't regret it. We're all going some, except you. You're going out on the old trail again - which begins in Third Avenue, and ends in Sing Sing. Why tear yourself away, Spike?"

Spike concentrated his gaze on a weedy young emigrant in a blue jersey, who was having his eye examined by the overworked doctor and seemed to be resenting it.

"Dere's nuttin' doin' dis side, boss," he said, at length. "I want to git busy."

"Ulysses Mullins!" said Jimmy, looking at him curiously. "I know the feeling. There's only one cure. I sketched it out for you once, but I guess you'll never take it. Yon don't think a lot of women, do you? You're the rugged bachelor."

"Goils - !" began Spike comprehensively, and abandoned the topic without dilating on it further.

Jimmy lighted his pipe, and threw the match overboard.

The sun came out from behind a cloud, and the water sparkled.

"Dose were great jools, boss," said Spike, thoughtfully.

"I believe you're still brooding over them, Spike."

"We could have got away wit' dem, if youse would have stood fer it. Dead easy."

"You are brooding over them. Spike, I'll tell you something which will console you a little, before you start out on your wanderings. It's in confidence, so keep it dark. That necklace was paste."

"What's dat?"

"Nothing but paste. I got next directly you handed them to me. They weren't worth a hundred dollars."

A light of understanding came into Spike's eyes. His face beamed with the smile of one to whom dark matters are made clear.

"So, dat's why you wouldn't stan' fer gittin' away wit' dem!" he exclaimed.

Printed in the United States
41695LVS00007B